RULES OF THUMB

A GUIDE FOR WRITERS

Fourth Edition

JAY SILVERMAN
Nassau Community College

ELAINE HUGHES
Nassau Community College

DIANA ROBERTS WIENBROER
Nassau Community College

Boston, MA   Burr Ridge, IL   Dubuque, IA   Madison, WI
New York, NY   San Francisco, CA   St. Louis, MO
Bangkok   Bogotá   Caracas   Lisbon   London   Madrid   Mexico City
Milan   New Delhi   Seoul   Singapore   Sydney   Taipei   Toronto

McGraw-Hill Higher Education

A Division of The **McGraw-Hill** *Companies*

RULES OF THUMB: A Guide for Writers

This book is printed on recycled, acid-free paper containing 10% postconsumer waste.

1 2 3 4 5 6 7 8 9 0 DOC/DOC 9 0 9 8 7 6 5 4 3 2 1 0 9

ISBN 0–07–229195–8 (text version)
ISBN 0–07–236333–9 (trade version)

Director and Publisher: *Phillip A. Butcher*
Senior sponsoring editor: *Lisa Moore*
Editorial assistant: *Emily Sparano*
Marketing manager: *Lesley Denton*
Project manager: *Christine Parker*
Production supervisor: *Michael R. McCormick*
Designer: *Pam Verros*
Supplement coordinator: *Nancy Martin*
Compositor: *Shepherd Incorporated*
Typeface: *11/13 Palatino*
Printer: *R. R. Donnelley & Sons Company*

The Library of Congress has catalogued an earlier version of this book as follows:

Silverman, Jay (XXX)
    Rules of thumb : a guide for writers / Jay Silverman, Elaine
Hughes, Diana Roberts Wienbroer. — 4th ed.
        p.   cm.
    Includes index.
    ISBN 0–07–092074–5 (acid-free paper)
    1. English language—Rhetoric.   2. English language—Grammar.
3. Report writing.   I. Hughes, Elaine.   II. Wienbroer, Diana
Roberts.   III. Title.
PE1408.S48781998
808'.042—dc21   97–43278

http://www.mhhe.com

CONTENTS

Acknowledgments   v
How to Use *Rules of Thumb*   vii

PART 1: CORRECTNESS

A Word About Correctness   2
Confusing Words [*to* and *too, their* and *there*]   3
One Word or Two? [*a lot*]   8
Spelling (*ie or ei?* One *p* or two?]   11
Capitalization   14
Abbreviations and Numbers   16
Apostrophes ['s]   18
Consistent Pronouns [*he or she, they, one*]   19
Correct Pronouns [*I* vs. *me*]   22
Vague Pronouns [*which, it, this, that,* and *who*]   24
Recognizing Complete Sentences   26
Sentence Fragments and Run-on Sentences   29
Commas [,]   35
Semicolons [;]   37
Colons [:]   38
Dashes and Parentheses [—( )]   39
Quotation Marks [" "]   41
Underlining or Quoting Titles   45
Verb Tenses   46
Shifting Verb Tenses [*moved, had moved*]   51
Verb Agreement   53
Word Endings: *s* and *ed*   54
Tangled Sentences [Parallel Structure, Danglers]   56

PART 2: PUTTING A PAPER TOGETHER

What to Do When You're Stuck   61
Finding an Organization for Your Essay   65
How to Work on a Second Draft   68
How to Make a Paper Longer (and When to Make It Shorter)   70
Introductions and Conclusions   72

Paragraphs—Long and Short   75
Transitions   78
Proofreading Tips   80

PART 3: MEETING SPECIFIC ASSIGNMENTS

Format of College Papers   85
Writing in Class   88
Writing About Literature   91
How to Quote From Your Sources   95
Using the College Library and the Internet   97
Writing Research Papers   104
Plagiarism (Cheating)   111
Documentation   112

PART 4: WRITING WITH ELEGANCE

Keeping a Journal   129
Finding Your Voice   132
Adding Details   133
Recognizing Clichés   135
Eliminating Biased Language   137
Trimming Wordiness   139
Varying Your Sentences   142

Postscript   147
About the Authors   148
Index   149

Acknowledgments

For their careful reading and questioning of various drafts of *Rules of Thumb*, we wish to thank Beverly Jensen; Polly Marshall, Hinds Community College; Nell Ann Pickett, Hinds Community College; and Larry Richman, Virginia Highlands Community College. Special thanks go to Sue Pohja, of Langenscheidt Publishers, Inc., whose enthusiasm for this book helped to create a trade edition. Tim Julet, our editor at McGraw-Hill, has both challenged and supported us in making the fourth edition the best one yet.

We are grateful for the encouragement and enthusiasm of our colleagues in the English Department at Nassau Community College. In particular, we wish to thank Paula Beck, James Blake, Mimi Quen Cheiken, Kathryn Tripp Feldman, Jeanne Hunter, Bernice Kliman, Hedda Marcus, Kathy McHale, John Tucker, Dominick Yezzo, and Scott Zaluda. Jeffrey Wohler, a student, asked valuable questions that improved this edition.

We also appreciate the thoughtful comments of Andrew J. Auge, Loras College; Doris Barkin, City College; Judy Bechtel, North Kentucky University; Michel de Benedictis, Miami Dade Community College; Michael Browner, Miami Dade Community College; Tim Bywater, Dixie College; Joseph T. Calabrese, University of Nevada; Robin Calitri, Merced College; Lawrence Carlson, Orange Coast College; Diana Cox, Amarillo College; Ralph G. Dille, University of Southern Colorado; Michael DiRaimo, Manchester Community College; Steffeny Fazzio, Salt Lake Community College; Susan Finlayson, Adirondack Community College; Ellen Gardiner, University of Mississippi; James F. Gerlach, Northwestern Michigan College; Matthew Goldie, NYCTC; Andrew Halford, Paducah Community College; Jacqueline Lautin, Hunter College; Mary McFarland, Fresno City College; Bonnie Plumber, Eastern Kentucky University; Sims Cheek Poindexter, Central Carolina Community

College; Retta Porter, Hinds Community College; Sara L. Sanders, Coastal Community College; Jeanne Smith, Oglala Lakota College; Stephen Straight, Manchester Community College; and A. Gordon Van Ness III, Longwood College.

This book would not have existed but for our students—both as the audience we had in mind and as perceptive readers and critics.

Jay Silverman
Elaine Hughes
Diana Roberts Wienbroer

How to Use *Rules of Thumb*

This book is for you if you love to write, but it's also for you if you *have* to write. *Rules of Thumb* is a quick guide that reduces each writing problem to a few practical points. You can use it easily, on your own, and feel confident in your writing.

We suggest that you read *Rules of Thumb* in small doses, out of order, when you need it. It's not like a novel that keeps you up late into the night. You'll need to read a few lines and then pause to see if you understand. After ten minutes, set the book aside. From time to time, look at the same points again as a reminder.

> Part 1, "Correctness," covers the most common mistakes. We put these rules first because they are what most students worry about and will want to have handy. However, when you are writing your ideas, don't get distracted with correctness; afterwards, take the time to look up the rules you need.

> Part 2, "Putting a Paper Together," takes you through the stages of writing an essay—from coming up with ideas to proofreading.

> Part 3, "Meeting Specific Assignments," offers help with writing under time pressure, as well as with writing literature papers and term papers.

> Part 4, "Writing with Elegance," offers ways to grow as a writer.

You won't necessarily use these parts in order because the process of writing does not follow a set sequence. Generating ideas, organizing, revising, and correcting all happen at several points along the way.

Rules of Thumb doesn't attempt to cover every little detail of grammar and usage, but it does cover the most common problems we've seen as teachers of writing over the past twenty-five years. We chose the phrase "rules of thumb" because it means a quick guide. The top part of your thumb is roughly an inch long. Sometimes you need a ruler, marked in millimeters, but sometimes you can do fine by measuring with just your thumb. Your thumb takes only a second to use, and it's always with you. We hope you'll find *Rules of Thumb* just as easy and comfortable to use.

> Jay Silverman
> Elaine Hughes
> Diana Roberts Wienbroer

PART 1

CORRECTNESS

A Word About Correctness
Confusing Words
One Word or Two?
Spelling
Capitalization
Abbreviations and Numbers
Apostrophes
Consistent Pronouns
Correct Pronouns
Vague Pronouns
Recognizing Complete Sentences
Sentence Fragments and Run-on Sentences
Commas
Semicolons
Colons
Dashes and Parentheses
Quotation Marks
Underlining or Quoting Titles
Verb Tenses
Shifting Verb Tenses
Verb Agreement
Word Endings: *s* and *ed*
Tangled Sentences

A WORD ABOUT CORRECTNESS

Too much concern about correctness can inhibit your writing; too little concern can come between you and your readers. Don't let the fear of errors dominate the experience of writing for you. On the other hand, we would be misleading you if we told you that correctness doesn't matter. Basic errors in writing will distract and turn off even the most determined readers. We encourage you to master the few rules presented here as quickly as possible so that you can feel secure about your writing. Once that happens, you'll be free to concentrate on what you want to say.

Confusing Words

These words are used all the time, so you need to know them. Find the ones that give you trouble and learn those.

a	Use before words starting with consonant sounds or long *u* (*a* bat, *a* coat, *a* union).
an	Use before words starting with vowels or pronounced as if they did (*an* age, *an* egg, *an* hour, *an* M&M).
accept	To take, to receive
	This office does not accept collect phone calls.
except	Not including
	Everybody except the piano player stopped playing.
affect	To change or influence
	Even nonprescription drugs can affect us in significant ways.
effect	The result, the consequence *Effect* is usually a noun, so you'll find *the* or *an* in front.
	Scientists have studied the effects of aspirin on heart disease.
conscience	The sense of right and wrong
	His conscience was clear.
conscious	Aware
	Flora became conscious of someone else in the room.
etc.	Abbreviation of *et cetera* (Latin for "and so forth"). The *c* is at the end, followed by a period. Don't write *and etc.*
	We bought beads, confetti, serpentine, fireworks, etc., for Mardi Gras.

good, well	Test by trying your sentence with both. If *well* fits, use it.
	Maybloom plays third base well.
	Maybloom is a good third baseman.

But note these tricky cases:

> Olivia looks good. (She's good-looking.)
>
> Rivka looks well. (She's no longer sick.)
>
> Clara sees well. (Her eyes work.)

it's	It is. Test by substituting *it is*.
	It's finished. It's time to go.
its	Possessive
	Every goat is attached to its own legs.

No apostrophe. *It is* cannot be substituted.

lay	To put something down
	-ing: She is laying the cards on the table.
	Past tense: He laid the cards on the table.

Once you *lay* something down, it *lies* there.

lie	To recline
	Aunt Pauline likes to lie down every afternoon.
	Past tense (here's the tricky part): *lay*
	Yesterday Aunt Pauline lay down for half an hour.

Lied always means "told a lie."

lying	Reclining
	The baby was lying on a pillow.
	Telling a lie
	They were lying to the news media.
loose	Not tight
	After he lost thirty pounds, his jeans were all loose.
lose	To misplace
	I constantly lose my glasses.
	To be defeated
	I win; you lose.
no, new, now, know, knew	*No* is negative; *new* is not old; *now* is the present moment. *Know* and *knew* refer to knowledge.
of, have	Remember: *could have, should have, would have*—or *would've*—not *would of*
passed	A course, a car, a football; also *passed away (died)*
	Kirtley passed me on the street; he also passed English.
	Saturday he passed for two touchdowns.
	The coach passed away.
past	Yesterdays (the past; past events); also, *beyond*
	Rousseau could never forget his past romances.
	You can't rewrite the past.
	Go two miles past the railroad tracks.

quiet	Spike Jones rarely played quiet music.
quit	Mrs. Salvatore quit her job the day she won the lottery.
quite	Hippos are quite fast, considering their bulk.
than	Comparison
	I'd rather dance than eat.
then	Next
	She then added a drop of water.
their	Something is theirs.
	They never checked their facts.
	Wild dogs care for their young communally.
there	*A place:* Go over there.
	There is . . . *There* are . . . *There* was . . . *There* were
	There are several theories to explain Napoleon's retreat.
they're	They are.
	They're trying hard to be polite.
to	*Direction:* Give it to me. Go to New York.
	A verb form: To see, to run, to be (Note that you barely pronounce *to.*)
too	*More than enough:* Too hot, too bad, too late, too much.
	Also: Me, too! (Note that you pronounce *too* clearly.)
two	2

were	*Past tense:* You were, we were, they were.
we're	*We are:* We're a nation of immigrants.
where	*A place:* Where were you when the lights went out?
whether	*If*—not *weather* (rain or snow)
	Please let me know whether you will be going.
who's	*Who is:* Who's there? Who's coming with us?
whose	*Possessive:* Whose diamond is this?
woman	One person
	The Board hired a woman for the job.
women	Several of them
	This woman is different from all other women.

Remember: *a* wom*a*n; *a* m*a*n

your	Belonging to you. Use only for your house, your car—*not* when you mean *you are.*
	That is your problem.
	Your socks should match.
you're	You are.
	You're going to question my logic.
	I'd like to know what you're thinking.

ONE WORD OR TWO?

If you can put another word between them, you'll know to keep them separate. Otherwise, you'll have to check them one by one.

a lot	I owe you a lot–a whole lot. (*A lot* is always written as two words.)
all ready	We were all ready for Grandpa's wedding.
already	Those crooks have already taken their percentage.
all right	It's all right with me if you want to call after midnight.
a long	Childhood seems like a long time.
along	They walked along the Navajo Trail.
a part	I want a part of the American pie.
apart	The twins were rarely apart.
at least	You'll need at least three disks for the computer.
each other	Frankie and Johnny can't stand to be away from each other.
even though	Even though I hate to garden, I love the flowers.
everybody	Everybody in the room danced frantically.
every day	It rains every day, every single day.
everyday	Fernando put on his everyday clothes.
every one	Every one of the beavers survived the flood.
everyone	Everyone likes pizza.
in depth	Study the biology textbook in depth.

in fact	In fact, Janine wasn't even in the room when the ruckus started.
in order	In order to prove his point, Mr. Baird climbed out the window.
in spite of	I like you in spite of your churlish disposition.
intact	She tried to keep her mind intact.
into	Ann Appleton fell into an easy job.
in touch	Please keep in touch with your sister.
itself	The snake wrapped itself around my neck.
myself	I took myself to the picture show.
nobody	Nobody knows how Mr. Avengail makes his money.
no one	No one on the staff speaks Spanish.
nowadays	Nowadays, they call iceboxes "refrigerators."
nevertheless	Nevertheless, the crew survived the crash.
somehow	Somehow no one proofread the newsletter.
some time sometimes	I need some time alone. Sometimes your mouth can get you into trouble.
throughout	Throughout the entire summer, David lounged on the beach.
whenever	Whenever I hear that song, I start to cry.

whereas	Horn-rimmed glasses are heavy whereas wire rims are light.
wherever	Wherever they go, photographers follow them.
withheld	The tenants withheld the rent because the roof leaked.
without	You'll never catch Pearl without her sunglasses.

Hyphenated Words

- Hyphens join compound words.

  self-employed
  in-laws
  seventy-five
  happy-go-lucky

- Hyphens make a two-word adjective before a noun, but not after it.

  Alfred Hitchcock is a well-known filmmaker.
  Alfred Hitchcock is well known as a filmmaker.

  George Eliot was a nineteenth-century author.
  George Eliot wrote in the nineteenth century.

Spelling

There's no getting around it. Correct spelling takes patience. But you can save time by learning the rules that fit your errors and by using a spellcheck on a computer.

I Before *E*

Use *I* before *E*
Except after *C*
Or when sounded like A
As in *neighbor* and *weigh.*

bel*i*eve	dece*i*ve	fre*i*ght
fr*i*end	rece*i*ve	ve*i*n
p*i*ece	conce*i*t	

Exceptions:

we*i*rd	fore*i*gn	le*i*sure	se*i*ze	the*i*r

Word Endings

The quiet *-ed* endings:

Three *-ed* endings are not always pronounced clearly, but they need to be written.

used to	supposed to	prejudiced

-sk and *-st* endings:

When *s* is added to words like these, it isn't always clearly pronounced, but it still needs to be there.

asks	consists	psychologists
risks	insists	scientists
desks	suggests	terrorists
tasks	costs	interests

The -*y* endings:

When a verb ends in *y*, keep the *y* when you add *ing*. To add *s* or *ed*, change the *y* to *i*.

crying	cries	cried
studying	studies	studied
trying	tries	tried

When a noun ends in *y*, make it plural by changing the *y* to *i* and adding *es*.

activities	families	theories

Exception: Simply add *s* to nouns ending in *ey*.

attorneys	monkeys	valleys

p or *pp*? t or *tt*?

Listen to the *vowel before* the added part.

If the vowel sounds like its own letter name, *use only one consonant:*

> writer   writing

The *i* sounds like the name of the letter *i*, so you use one *t*.

If the vowel before the added part has a different sound from its name, *double the consonant:*

> written

The *i* sounds like the *i* in *it*, so you double the *t*.

The same method works for *hoping* and *hopping*. Listen for the different sounds of the letter *o*.

Here are some other examples:

beginning	dropping	quitting
stopped	occurred	referred

An exception: *coming*

Words with Prefixes and Suffixes

When you add a prefix or suffix, you usually keep the spelling of the root word.

*mis*spell	sudden*ness*	*dis*satisfaction
hope*ful*	*dis*appear	govern*ment*
*un*noticed	environ*ment*	

The *-ly* endings also follow this rule.

really   totally   lonely   finally   unfortunately

But *truly* does not follow the rule.

Exception: The final *e* is usually dropped before a suffix that starts with a vowel.

debat*able*   sens*ible*   lov*able*

Tricky Words

Look hard at the middle of each word:

de*finite*ly	em*bar*rass	usu*al*ly
se*par*ate	ac*comm*odate	ne*cess*ary
re*peti*tion	pro*bab*ly	fam*il*iar
o*pin*ion	in*ter*est	

Tips for Becoming a Better Speller

- Use a computer spellcheck every time you edit or revise your paper; remember, however, that a spellcheck won't catch commonly confused words or incorrect word endings.

- Keep an ongoing list of every word you misspell. Study the list once a week.

- Write three times any word you misspell, and then add it to your list.

- Sound out words. Use your hearing to help you spell words syllable by syllable.

- Make a habit of using your dictionary.

Capitalization

Capitalize the first letter of every sentence and of names of people, localities, days of the week, and months. Do not capitalize for emphasis.

Do Capitalize

- Subjects in school whose names come from names of countries; complete titles of courses

    English   Spanish   History 101

- In titles, the first word, major words, and words of five letters or more

    The Red and the Black   *All About Eve*

- Family names like *Mother, Aunt,* or *Grandfather* only when used as a name or with a name (but not after *my, his, her, their, our*)

    Papa was cared for by Uncle Manny after my mother left.

- Days of the week

    Wednesday   Saturday

- People's titles when they precede their names

    Dr. Judd   Officer Zublonski   Major Gross

- Brand names

    Kleenex   Coca-Cola   Domino's Pizza

- Public holidays

    Thanksgiving   Fourth of July

- The entire name of a specific place, event, etc.

    Oak Street   Battle of Gettysburg   Calhoun High School

Do Not Capitalize

- Subjects in school whose names do not come from the names of countries

    history   psychology   marketing

- Genres of literature and art

    novel   poetry   gangster movies   jazz

- Family names like *mother, aunt, grandfather* after *a, the, my, his, her, their, our*

    my mother   his aunt   the grandmother

- Seasons of the year

    spring   autumn

- Titles of people separate from their names

    I went to the doctor.
    Two generals and an admiral were consulted.

- Generic names

    facial tissues   soda pop   pizza

- Private celebrations

    birthday   anniversary

- A type of place, event, etc.

    a dark street   the eve of battle   high school

- For emphasis

    Do not capitalize whole words (AMNESIA); do not capitalize an entire essay or Internet message.

ABBREVIATIONS AND NUMBERS

Avoid abbreviations, except for words that are always abbreviated. Spell out numbers that take only a word or two.

◾ ABBREVIATIONS

- As a general rule, don't abbreviate—especially don't use abbreviations like these in your papers:

dept.	yr.	NY	Eng.	Thurs.	b / c
w / o	co.	&	gov't.	Prof.	thru

- But do abbreviate words that you *always* see abbreviated—such as certain titles with proper names and well-known organizations:

Mr. Smith	FBI
St. Bartholomew	IBM

- Abbreviate *doctor* only before a name:

  the doctor   Dr. Salk

◾ NUMBERS

Spell Out

- Numbers that take only one or two words

  nine   twenty-seven   two billion

- Numbers that begin a sentence

  One hundred four years ago the ship sank.
  The ship sank 104 years ago.

- Numbers that form a compound word

  a two-year-old baby

- Fractions

  one-half

Use Numerals for

- Numbers that require three or more words

  1,889   162

- Dates, page references, room numbers, statistics, addresses, percentages, and dollars and cents

May 6, 1974	7,500 residents	99.44%
page 2	221 B Baker Street	$5.98

- A list or series of numbers

  1, 4, 9, 16, 25
  seats 12, 14, and 16

APOSTROPHES

Most of the time, when you add an *s* to a word you don't need an apostrophe. Use apostrophes for contractions and possessives.

Do Not Add an Apostrophe; Just Add *s* or *es*

To make a plural

Two bosses   Three dogs   Five families

To a present-tense verb

He sees.   She says.   It talks.   Carol sings.

Look hard at *sees* and *says:* no apostrophe.

Add an Apostrophe

To a contraction (put the apostrophe where the missing letter was)

doesn't = does not	it's = it is	that's
don't	I'm	weren't
didn't	you're	what's

To a possessive

Dagmar's hat	Baldwin's style	a night's sleep
Gus's hair	children's toys	a family's history
Ms. Jones's opinion	women's room	today's world

- If the word is plural and already ends with *s,* just add an apostrophe after the *s.*

    my friends' apartment (several friends)

    my grandparents' dishes

- Pronouns in possessive form have *no* apostrophe.

    its   hers   his   ours   theirs   yours

Consistent Pronouns

Make a conscious choice of your pronouns. Don't shift from *a person* to *they* to *you* to *I.*

The problem comes with sentences like

> I got mad; it does make you feel upset when people don't listen.

> A young person has to manage their time well if they want to get ahead.

Study the following options:

*a person
. . . they*

> *A person* or *someone* when used with *they* or *their* causes the most trouble with consistency. *A person* and *someone* are singular; *they* and *their* are plural. Mixing these words in one sentence leads to awkward writing and creates errors.

>> If a person knows what they want, they can be firm.

>> I know someone rich, and they are not very happy.

> Nowadays you will hear this usage in conversation and will even see it in print, but it is still not acceptable in most writing.

> Instead of *a person* or *someone,* try *people* (which fits with *they*).

>> When people know what they want, they can be firm.

> Or better yet, use a true-to-life example, a real person.

>> My cousin Marc is rich, but he is not very happy.

> A real example not only makes the grammar correct, but it is also much more interesting and memorable. *A person* and *someone* are nobodies.

he,
he or she

The old-fashioned pronoun choice to accompany *a person* is *he.*

> When a person is not afraid of criticism,
> he can be a bold writer.

But this choice presumes that *a person* is male. It should be avoided because it is sexist language. *He or she* is possible, but not if it comes several times in a row; *he or she,* when repeated, becomes clunky and awkward.

> When a person is not afraid of criticism,
> he or she will not worry about what
> others think of him or her.

Avoid *he/she* and *s/he.* The best solution, often, is to use plurals such as *people* and *they.*

> When people are not afraid of criticism,
> they can be bold writers.

I

Don't be afraid of *I.* It is very strong in writing about emotions and experience. In these matters, being objective is not as good as being truthful. As Thoreau wrote, "I should not talk so much about myself if there were anybody else whom I knew as well." A lot of times when you generalize, you really are writing from experience. If you speak for yourself, often you will get to the nitty-gritty of the subject—what you know to be true.

> If I were not afraid of criticism, I could be
> a bold writer.

> When I am not afraid of criticism, I am a
> bold writer.

You don't, however, need phrases like *I think* or *in my opinion* because the whole paper is, after all, what you choose to say.

you	*You* is good for giving directions and writing letters. It establishes an intimate tone with your reader. For essays, however, it may seem too informal or too preachy.

> If you are not afraid of criticism, you can be a bold writer.

Try *we* instead, when you mean *people in general*.

> If we are not afraid of criticism, we can be bold writers.

In any case, beware of mixing pronouns.

> Riding my bicycle is good for your legs.

one	*One* means a person—singular. If you use it, you must stick with it.

> When one is not afraid of criticism, one can be a bold writer.

One is an option for solving the *he/she* problem; it is appropriate for formal writing. Nevertheless, when repeated, *one* can sound stuffy. How many times can one say *one* before one makes oneself sound silly?

we	*We* can be used to mean *people in general*.

> When we are not afraid of criticism, we can be bold writers.

Be careful that you mean more than just yourself. Using *I* might be more appropriate.

they	*They* is often the best solution to the *he/she* problem, but remember that *they* must refer to a plural, such as *many people* or *some people*.

> When people are not afraid of criticism, they can be bold writers.

no pronoun	Often you can avoid the problem entirely.

Instead of

> A young person has to manage his or her time well if he or she wants to get ahead.

write:

> A young person has to manage time well to get ahead.
>
> A writer who is not afraid of criticism is a bold writer.

CORRECT PRONOUNS

I, she, he, we, they, and *who* identify the persons doing the action. *Me, her, him, us, them,* and *whom* identify the persons receiving the action.

Pairs: My Friends and I / My Friends and Me

- With a pair of people, try the sentence without the other person:

    > My friends and I saw the movie six times.
    > (. . . I saw the movie, *not* Me saw the movie.)

    > Carter gave the tickets to my friends and me.
    > (Carter gave the tickets to me, *not* to I.)

The same rule goes for *him, her, he, she.*

> The friar mixed a potion for Romeo and her.
> (He mixed the potion for her, *not* for she.)

Note: Put yourself last in a list:

> My friends and I saw the movie.
> (*Not* Me and my friends saw the movie.)

> Beverly gave pumpkin cake to Noah, Hannah, and me.

Don't be afraid of *me;* it's often right.

> Between you and me, Mickey is heading for a fall.
> (*Not* Between you and I . . .)

- Don't use *myself* when *me* will do.

> I did the typing myself.
> (Here, *me* cannot be substituted.)

> Sam did the typing for Toby and me.
> (*Not* . . . for Toby and myself.)

Never write *themself;* use *themselves.*

Comparisons

- Use *I, he, she, we, they* when comparing with the subject of the sentence—usually the first person in the sentence.

> Phil was kinder to Sarah than I was.
> Zachary is more nervous than she is.

Sometimes *is* is left off the end:

> Zachary is more nervous than she.

- Use *me, him, her, us, them* when comparing with the receiver, the object of the sentence—usually the person mentioned later in the sentence.

> Phil was kinder to Sarah than to me.

Note the difference:

> He was nastier to Ramona than I.

(He was nastier to Ramona than I was.)

> He was nastier to Ramona than me.

(He was nastier to Ramona than to me.)

Who / Whom

- Use *whom* after prepositions (to whom, of whom, for whom, from whom, with whom).

> To whom should I address my complaint?

- Use *who* for subjects of verbs.

> Who should I say is calling?

When in doubt, use *who*.

VAGUE PRONOUNS

Certain pronouns–*which, it, this, that,* and *who*–must refer to a single word, not to a whole phrase. Keep them near the word they refer to.

These words are used loosely in conversation, but in most writing you should use them more precisely.

Which

Which causes the most trouble of the five. Don't overuse it.

> *Imprecise:* Last week I felt sick in which I didn't even get to go to school.
>
> *Precise:* Last week I felt sick. I didn't even get to go to school.
>
> *Precise:* Last week I had a cold which kept me from going to school.

In the last example, *which* clearly refers to *cold.*

Use *in which* only when you mean that one thing is inside the other:

> The box in which I keep my jewelry fell apart.

Note that *which* normally cannot start a sentence unless it asks a question.

It

When you use *it,* make sure the reader knows what *it* is. *It* is often weak at the start of a sentence when *it* refers to nothing.

> *Imprecise:* Eleanore ate a big Chinese dinner and then had a chocolate milkshake for dessert. *It* made her sick.
>
> *Precise:* Eleanore ate a big Chinese dinner and then had a chocolate milkshake for dessert. The *combination* made her sick.

This

This cannot refer to a whole situation or a group of things, so insert a word after *this* to sum up what *this* refers to.

> *Imprecise:* She never calls me, she's never ready when I pick her up for a date, and she forgot my birthday. *This* makes me angry.

> *Precise:* She never calls me, she's never ready when I pick her up for a date, and she forgot my birthday. This *behavior* makes me angry.

That

Just like *this, that* cannot refer to a whole situation or a group of things. When *that* seems unclear, replace it with what it stands for.

> *Imprecise:* We are not paid well and receive inadequate benefits, but I don't think we should discuss *that* yet.

The reader might ask, "Discuss *what* yet?"

> *Precise:* We are not paid well and receive inadequate benefits, but I don't think we should discuss *benefits* yet.

Who

Use *who* for people—not *which.*

> The runner who finished last got all the publicity.

Recognizing Complete Sentences

At the heart of every sentence—no matter how complicated—is a subject-verb combination.

To recognize a complete sentence, you need to recognize its true subject and verb.

☐ Simple Sentences

- A sentence always has a *subject* and a *verb:*

      I won.
      Phillippe snores.
      This soup is cold.

  I, Phillippe, soup are the subjects; *won, snores, is* are the verbs. Notice that the verb enables the subject to *do* or *be* something.

  These very short sentences have only a one-word subject and a one-word verb.

- Usually a word or phrase completes the subject and verb:

      Janeen walks three miles a day.

      Suzanne spent all of her savings.

      It's not very difficult.

      She says absolutely nothing.

      They had headaches for two days.

      Robert is my latest fiancé.

      The "blow torch murders" were committed by the least likely suspect—the grandmother.

      High above the Kona coast in Hawaii stands one of the world's great chocolate plantations.

- Sentences can have more than one subject and more than one verb:

    Tracy and Pete have a new home. (two subjects)

    They bought an old house and restored it. (two verbs)

- Sometimes the subject is understood to be "you," the reader; the sentence is usually a command or a direction:

    Avoid submerging this product in water.

    Walk two blocks past the traffic light.

- Sometimes a word or group of words introduces the main part of a sentence:

    However, the bar is closed.

    For example, chemists write CO_2 instead of *carbon dioxide.*

    Then we drove a thousand miles.

    At the end of the game, the umpire and the pitcher got into a fight.

    In the cabin by the lake, you'll find the paddles and life jackets.

For more information about recognizing subjects and verbs, see "Verb Agreement," page 53.

■ COMPOUND OR COORDINATE SENTENCES

Two complete sentences can be joined to make a *compound,* or *coordinate,* sentence.

- Sometimes the two sentences are joined by a comma and one of the following connecting words:

and	so	or	for
but	yet	nor	

    Janeen walks three miles a day, but she still eats junk food.

    Suzanne spent all of her savings, and now she has to start using her credit cards.

- Sometimes the two sentences are connected by a semicolon.

    Grasshoppers are lazy; they are not very hard to catch.

■ COMPLEX OR SUBORDINATE SENTENCES

Sometimes a sentence has two parts—the main part (a complete short sentence) and a *subordinated* part (a complete short sentence preceded by a *subordinating* word, such as *because, although, if, when, after,* or *while*).

> Suzanne has spent all of her savings because her brother is ill.
>
> Mona shouts when she talks on the telephone.
>
> The primary market for sea urchins is Japan although they are harvested in Maine.

Notice in the first sentence that "Suzanne has spent all of her savings" could be a complete sentence. On the other hand, "because her brother is ill" is not complete by itself. In the second sentence, "when she talks on the telephone" is also incomplete. In the third sentence, "although they are harvested in Maine" is incomplete.

The two parts of each sentence are reversible:

> Because her brother is ill, Suzanne has spent all of her savings.
>
> When she talks on the telephone, Mona shouts.
>
> Although sea urchins are harvested in Maine, the primary market is Japan.

A *compound-complex sentence* occurs when one or both halves of a compound sentence have subordinated parts.

> Suzanne always seemed to be a skinflint, but she has spent all her savings because her brother is ill.

SENTENCE FRAGMENTS AND RUN-ON SENTENCES

To decide whether to use a period or a comma, look at what comes before and after the punctuation.

Often you reach a pause in your writing, and you wonder, "Do I put a comma or a period?" The length of a sentence has nothing to do with the right choice. You need to look at what comes before and after the punctuation to see whether you have two separate sentences or a single sentence with a fragment attached to it.

■ RECOGNIZING SENTENCE FRAGMENTS

Many sentence fragments may appear to be complete sentences, but they have elements that make them incomplete.

Words That Rarely Begin Sentences

Certain words *almost never* begin sentences:

such as	which	
especially	who	
not	whose	except in a question
like, just like	how	
the same as	what	

In addition, if you have trouble with sentence fragments, it's best not to start sentences with *and* or *but*.

In most cases, put a comma or a dash before these words.

Incorrect: We had to drain the pipes after every vacation. Especially in the winter.

Correct: We had to drain the pipes after every vacation—especially in the winter.

Incorrect: They gave me one lousy dollar. Which was a full day's pay.

Correct: They gave me one lousy dollar, which was a full day's pay.

Incorrect: N. C. Wyeth illustrated many children's books. Such as Jules Verne's *The Mysterious Island.*

Correct: N. C. Wyeth illustrated many children's books, such as Jules Verne's *The Mysterious Island.*

Subordinating Words

Certain words always begin *half* a sentence—either the first half or the second half. These are called *subordinating words:*

when	if
before	because
after	although (even though)
as	unless
while	whereas

A sentence fragment frequently begins with a subordinating word.

Incorrect: Although Janeen walks three miles a day.

When Archduke Franz Ferdinand was assassinated in Sarajevo.

You can fix these fragments by connecting each fragment to the sentence before or after it.

Correct: Although Janeen walks three miles a day, she still has to watch her diet.

Janeen still has to watch her diet although she walks three miles a day.

When Archduke Franz Ferdinand was assassinated in Sarajevo, the whole world was plunged into war.

The whole world was plunged into war when Archduke Franz Ferdinand was assassinated in Sarajevo.

You can also drop the subordinating word.

Correct: Janeen walks three miles a day.

Archduke Franz Ferdinand was assassinated in Sarajevo.

A subtle point: Watch out for *and*. Putting *and* between a fragment and a sentence doesn't fix the fragment.

> *Still*
> *Incorrect:* Although Janeen walks three miles a day and she still watches her diet.

> *Correct:* Although Janeen walks three miles a day and she still watches her diet, she has not yet reached her goal.

Verbs Ending in *-ing*

Verbs ending in *-ing* cannot serve as the main verb of a sentence:

> *Incorrect:* The boys ran toward the ocean. Leaping across the hot sand.

> I have three good friends. One being my cousin.

> I love walking in the evening and taking in nature's beauty. The sun setting over the prairie. The wind blowing the tall grass.

One solution is to connect the fragment to the preceding sentence.

> *Correct:* The boys ran toward the ocean, leaping across the hot sand.

> I love walking in the evening and taking in nature's beauty— the sun setting over the prairie and the wind blowing the tall grass.

The second solution is to change the *-ing* verb to a complete verb.

> *Correct:* They leaped across the hot sand.
> One is my cousin.

An *-ing* verb *can* begin a sentence if a complete verb comes later.

> *Correct:* Leaping across the hot sand hurts my feet.

To Verbs

To verbs *(to be, to feel)* also frequently begin fragments.

> *Incorrect:* I went back home to talk to my father. To tell him how I feel.

> Keep this hairdryer away from the sink. To avoid submersion in water.

Fix these fragments by connecting them to the sentence before or by adding a subject and verb:

Correct: I went back home to talk to my father, to tell him how I feel.

I went back home to talk to my father. I needed to tell him how I feel.

Keep this hairdryer away from the sink to avoid submersion in water.

Keep this hairdryer away from the sink. You must avoid submerging it in water.

A *to* verb can begin a sentence if a complete verb comes later.

Correct: To talk to my father always calms me down.

Repeated Words

A repeated word can create a fragment.

Incorrect: Elizabeth's the ideal cat. A cat who both plays and purrs.

I believe that Whitman is our greatest poet. That he singlehandedly began modern American poetry.

The best solution here is to replace the period with a comma.

Correct: Elizabeth's the ideal cat, a cat who both plays and purrs.

I believe that Whitman is our greatest poet, that he singlehandedly began modern American poetry.

Note: *That* rarely begins a sentence, except when it points, as in "That was the year of the great flood."

Using Fragments for Style

You will notice that professional writers sometimes use sentence fragments for emphasis or style. Be sure you have control over fragments before you experiment. In the right spot, a fragment can be very strong.

▣ Recognizing Run–on Sentences

A run-on sentence happens when you have two complete sentences, but you have only a comma or no punctuation between them. Run-ons usually occur because the two sentences are closely related. The two most common spots where run-ons occur are

- When a pronoun begins the second sentence:

    Incorrect: The light floated toward us, it gave an eerie glow.

    Correct: The light floated toward us. It gave an eerie glow.

    Incorrect: Ralph decided to move to Paris, he wanted to be a writer.

    Correct: Ralph decided to move to Paris. He wanted to be a writer.

- When *however* begins the second sentence:

    Incorrect: Mosquitoes in the United States are just an annoyance, however in many countries they are a health hazard.

    Correct: Mosquitoes in the United States are just an annoyance. However, in many countries they are a health hazard.

How to Fix Run-on Sentences

Incorrect: I went to Gorman's Ice Cream Parlor, I ordered a triple hot fudge sundae.

Suzanne spent all of her savings now she is flat broke.

- The simplest way to fix a run-on sentence is to put a period or semicolon between the two sentences:

    Correct: I went to Gorman's Ice Cream Parlor. I ordered a triple hot fudge sundae.

    Suzanne spent all of her savings. Now she is flat broke.

(Remember that it is perfectly correct to have two or three short sentences in a row.)

Correct: I went to Gorman's Ice Cream Parlor; I ordered a triple hot fudge sundae.

Suzanne spent all of her savings; now she is flat broke.

- Here are two other ways to fix run-on sentences:

Put a comma and a conjunction between the two sentences. The conjunctions are *and, but, so, yet, for, or,* and *nor.*

Correct: I went to Gorman's Ice Cream Parlor, and I ordered a triple hot fudge sundae.

Suzanne spent all of her savings, so now she is flat broke.

Use a subordinating word with one of the sentences:

Correct: I went to Gorman's Ice Cream Parlor, where I ordered a triple hot fudge sundae.

Because Suzanne spent all of her savings, now she is flat broke.

■ USING *BUT, HOWEVER, ALTHOUGH*

These three words are used to reverse the meaning of a sentence, but they are punctuated differently.

These three words are used to reverse the meaning of a sentence; however, they are punctuated differently.

These three words are used to reverse the meaning of a sentence although they are punctuated differently.

COMMAS

You don't need a comma every time you breathe. Here are four places you need them.

Comma before *but, and, so, yet, or, for,* and *nor*

Put a comma before *but, and, so, yet, or, for,* and *nor* when they connect two sentences.

> The lead actor was on crutches, but the show went on.
>
> Gina intended to win the weight-lifting pageant, and that's exactly what she did.
>
> Not only did Melva run a restaurant, but she also wrote a cookbook.
>
> The house didn't sell at $300,000, so they lowered the price.

However, don't automatically stick in a comma just because a sentence is long.

> The short man smoking a cigar and shouting at the hostess is my uncle Jules.

Commas in a List or Series

Use commas between parts of a series of three or more.

> In one month the game farm saved the lives of a red fox, a great-horned owl, and a black bear cub.
>
> Diamond climbed up the ladder, marched to the end of the diving board, took a big spring, and came down in a belly bust.
>
> In the class sat a bearded man, a police officer, a woman eating a sandwich, and a parakeet.

(Without the last comma, what happens to the parakeet?)

Don't use a comma in a pair.

> In one month the game farm saved the lives of a red fox and a great-horned owl.
>
> Mary Ellen's mother handed out hard candies and made us sit while she played Mozart's "Turkish March" on the piano.

Comma after a Lead-in

Use a comma after an introductory part of a sentence.

> However, the truth finally came out.
>
> For example, you can learn how to fix a leaky faucet.
>
> After lunch, she gave me a cup of that terrible herb tea.
>
> When James walked in, the whole family was laughing hysterically.

A Pair of Commas around an Insertion

Surround an insertion or interruption with a *pair* of commas. Both commas are necessary.

> The truth, however, finally came out.
>
> Woody Guthrie, the father of Arlo Guthrie, wrote "This Land Is Your Land."
>
> My cousin, who thinks she is always right, was dead wrong.
>
> Milton, even though no one had invited him, arrived first at the party.
>
> In "The Raven," by Edgar Allen Poe, the bird gradually takes on more and more meaning for the narrator.

Note in the last example that the comma goes inside the quotation marks.

Places and *dates* are treated as insertions. Note especially that commas surround the year and the state.

> The hospital was in Oshkosh, Wisconsin, not far from Omro.
> I was born on August 15, 1954, at seven in the morning.

SEMICOLONS

Semicolons can be used instead of periods; they also can separate parts of a complicated list.

- Use a semicolon to connect two related sentences; each half must be a complete sentence.

    Ask for what you want; accept what you get.

    One day she says she's at death's door; the next day she's ready to rock and roll.

    I'll never forget the day of the circus; that's when I met the trapeze artist who changed my life.

    It's not that O'Hara's position is wrong; it's that he misses the key point.

    A semicolon often comes before certain transition words; a comma follows the transition.

however	therefore	otherwise
nevertheless	in other words	instead
for example	on the other hand	meanwhile
besides	furthermore	unfortunately

    Schubert was a great composer; however, Beethoven was greater.

    The bank lost two of my deposits; therefore, I am closing my account.

    Semicolons work best when used to emphasize a strong connection between the two sentences.

- Use semicolons instead of commas in a list when some of the parts already have commas.

    To make it as an actor, you need, first of all, some natural talent; second, the habits of discipline and concentration; and third, the ability to promote yourself.

Colons

Colons create suspense: they can set up a list, a quotation, or an emphatic statement.

Use a colon after a complete sentence to introduce related details.

Before a colon you must have a *complete statement*. Don't use a colon after *are* or *include* or *such as*.

Colons can introduce

- A list

    I came home loaded with supplies: a tent, a sleeping bag, and a pack.

- A quotation

    The author begins with a shocker: "Mother spent her summer sitting naked on a rock."

- An example

    I love to eat legumes: for example, beans or lentils.

- An emphatic assertion

    This is the bottom line: I refuse to work for only $5.00 an hour.

- A subtitle

    Rules of Thumb: A Guide for Writers

When you type, leave two spaces after a colon.

Dashes and Parentheses

Dashes and parentheses separate a word or remark from the rest of the sentence.

■ Dashes

Dashes highlight the part of the sentence they separate, or show an abrupt change of thought in mid-sentence, or connect a fragment to a sentence.

> Alberta Hunter—still singing at the age of eighty—performed nightly at The Cookery in New York City.
>
> At night the forest is magical and fascinating—and yet it terrifies me.
>
> Living the high life—that's what I want.

Dashes are very handy; they can replace a period, comma, colon, or semicolon. However, they are usually informal, so don't use many—or you will seem to have dashed off your paper.

When you type, two hyphens make a dash; there is no space before or after the dash.

■ Parentheses

Parentheses deemphasize the words they separate. Use them to enclose brief explanations or interruptions. They can contain either part of a sentence or a whole sentence.

> I demanded a reasonable sum ($10.50 an hour), and they met my request.
>
> Bergman's last film disappointed the critics. (See the attached reviews.)
>
> Mayme drives slowly (she claims her car won't go over forty miles per hour), so she gets tickets for causing traffic jams.

- Put any necessary punctuation *after* the second parenthesis if the parentheses contain part of a sentence.

- If the parentheses contain a complete sentence, put the period *inside* the second parenthesis. Notice, however, that you don't capitalize or use a period when parentheses enclose a sentence within a sentence.

Be sparing with parentheses. Too many can chop up your sentences.

Quotation Marks

Use quotation marks any time you use someone else's exact words. If they are not the exact words, don't surround them with quotation marks.

Quotations in this chapter come from the following selection from Mark Twain's *Adventures of Huckleberry Finn:*

> Sometimes we'd have the whole river all to ourselves for the longest time. Yonder was the banks and the islands, across the water; and maybe a spark—which was a candle in a cabin window—and sometimes on the water you could see a spark or two—on a raft or a scow, you know; and maybe you could hear a fiddle or a song coming over from one of them crafts. It's lovely to live on a raft.

Punctuation before a Quotation

Here are three ways to lead into a quotation:

- For short quotations (a word or a phrase), don't use *Twain says,* and don't put a comma before the quotation. Simply use the writer's phrase as it fits smoothly into your sentence:

  > Huck Finn finds it "lovely" to float down the Mississippi River on a raft.

- Put a comma before the quotation marks if you use *he says.* Put no comma if you use *he says that.*

  > Huck says, "It's lovely to live on a raft."
  > Huck says that "It's lovely to live on a raft."

- Use a colon (:) before a quotation of a sentence or more. Be sure you have a complete statement before the colon. Don't use *he says.*

  > In one short sentence, Twain pulls together the whole paragraph: "It's lovely to live on a raft."

Punctuation after a Quotation

At the end of a quotation, the period or comma goes *inside* the quotation marks. Do not close the quotation marks until the person's words end. Use one mark of punctuation to end your sentence— never two periods or a comma and a period.

> Twain writes, ". . . you could hear a fiddle or a song coming over from one of them crafts. It's lovely to live on a raft."

Semicolons go outside of closing quotation marks.

> Huck says, "It's lovely to live on a raft"; however, this raft eventually drifts him into trouble.

Question marks and exclamation marks go inside if the person you are writing about is asking or exclaiming. (If *you* are asking or exclaiming, the mark goes outside.)

> "Have you read *Huckleberry Finn*?" she asked.
> Did Twain call Huck's life "lovely"?

When your quotation is more than a few words, let the quotation end your sentence. Otherwise you're liable to get a tangled sentence.

> *Tangled:* Huck says, "It's lovely to live on a raft" illustrates his love of freedom.

> *Correct:* Huck says, "It's lovely to live on a raft." This quotation illustrates his love of freedom.

(See page 113 for a discussion of punctuation after quotations in research papers.)

Indenting Long Quotations

Long quotations (three or more lines) do not get quotation marks. Instead, start on a new line and indent the whole left margin of the quotation ten spaces. After the quotation, return to the original margin and continue your paragraph.

> Huck and Jim lead a life of ease:
>> Sometimes we'd have the whole river all to ourselves for the longest time. Yonder was the banks and the islands, across the water; and maybe a spark—which was a candle in a cabin window—and sometimes on

> the water you could see a spark or two—on a raft or a
> scow, you know; and maybe you could hear a fiddle or
> a song coming over from one of them crafts. It's lovely
> to live on a raft.

Brackets indicate that you have added or changed a word to make
the quotation clear.

An ellipsis (three periods separated by spaces) within brackets
indicates that you have left out words from the original quotation.
Use a fourth period after the brackets to end your sentence.

> Sometimes we'd have that whole river [the
> Mississippi] all to ourselves for the longest
> time [. . .]. It's lovely to live on a raft.

Dialogue

In dialogue, start a new paragraph every time you switch from one
speaker to the other.

> "Did you enjoy reading *Huckleberry Finn?*" asked Professor
> Migliaccio.
> "I guess so," Joylene said, "but the grammar is awful."
> The professor thought a moment. "You know, the book was
> once banned in Boston because of that. I guess Twain's
> experiment still has some shock value."
> "Well, it shocked me," said Joylene. "I can't believe an
> educated man would write that way."

Writing About a Word or Phrase

When you discuss a word or phrase, surround it with quotation
marks.

> The name "Mark Twain" means "two fathoms deep."

> Advertisers use "America," while news reporters refer to "the
> United States."

Do not use quotation marks around slang; either use the word
without quotation marks or find a better word.

Quotation within a Quotation

For quotations within a quotation, use single quotation marks:

> According to radio announcer Rhingo Lake, "The jockey clearly screamed 'I've been foiled!' as the horse fell to the ground right before the finish line."

Quoting Poetry

For poetry, when quoting two or more lines, indent ten spaces from the left margin and copy the lines of poetry exactly as the poet arranged them.

> We are such stuff
> As dreams are made on; and our little life
> Is rounded with a sleep.

When a line of poetry is too long to fit on a line of your paper, indent the turnover line an additional three spaces, as in the following line from Walt Whitman's *Leaves of Grass.*

> I believe that a leaf of grass is no less than the journeywork
> of the stars.

When quoting a *few* words of poetry that include a line break, use a slash mark to show where the poet's line ends.

> In *The Tempest*, Shakespeare calls us "such stuff / As dreams are made on. . . ."

Underlining or Quoting Titles

Underline titles of longer works and use quotation marks for titles of shorter works.

- Underline or *italicize* titles of longer works, such as books, magazines, plays, newspapers, movies, and television programs.

Newsweek	Saturday Night Live
The New York Times	The Wizard of Oz
War and Peace	Hamlet

  Use either underlining or italics, but don't mix them in your paper.

- Put "quotation marks" around titles of shorter works, such as short stories, articles, poems, songs, and chapter titles.

  "The Star-Spangled Banner"

  "The Pit and the Pendulum"

  Remember that a comma or period, if needed, goes inside the quotation marks.

  In "Stopping by Woods on a Snowy Evening," Robert Frost uses an intricate rhyme scheme.

- Do not underline or place quotation marks around your title on a cover sheet—unless your title contains someone else's title.

  My Week on a Shrimp Boat

  An Analysis of T. S. Eliot's "The Love Song of J. Alfred Prufrock"

  The Vision of War in The Red Badge of Courage

- Capitalize only the first word and all major words in a title.

Verb Tenses

Verb tenses indicate the level of time and duration of the events you describe. By changing the tense, you change the time—and therefore the meaning—of what happens in your sentence.

To see the difference that verb tenses make, look at what happens to the time of the action in these sentences:

> I *eat* at eleven o'clock.
> I *ate* at eleven o'clock.
> I *will eat* at eleven o'clock.

The clock time is the same; the time of the sentence changes.

■ Present, Past, Future

English has an astounding variety of ways to express time. Verb tenses can give you great power to say exactly what you mean, but they can also give you a big headache. Here are the most commonly used forms.

PRESENT TENSES

- Use present tense when you're generalizing, stating a fact, describing an ongoing action, or relating an incident in film or literature.

    > E-mail makes correspondence easier.
    >
    > Iguanas are reptiles.
    >
    > I eat at Levy's every Friday.
    >
    > Don Quixote holds a vigil in the barnyard.

- When describing an event occurring at the moment, normally use a *being* verb plus an *-ing* verb. (However, in writing you'll use this tense for very specific purposes—in journal and letter writing or for artistic effect.)

    > I am putting on my shoes.
    >
    > The king is counting out his money.
    >
    > Jeffrey is having a temper tantrum.

PAST TENSES

Simple

- When narrating an event that happened once, use the simple past tense.

    Jackson hit a home run in the sixth inning.

    I ran into my room and slammed the door.

- For a state of being in the past, use *was* or *were.*

    Noah was the tallest in his class.

- For events that went on for a period of time, use the past tense plus a phrase that indicates time or use *would* or *used to.*

    Uncle Harry walked to school every day.

    Uncle Harry would walk to school.

    Uncle Harry used to walk to school.

Note that following *would* and *used to,* the verb *walk* does not have an -*ed* ending.

Past Tense with *has, have,* and *had*

- For the past continuing up to the present, use *has* or *have* plus the past participle—usually an -*ed* ending.

    Open heart surgery has saved countless lives.

    Ed's three aunts have lived in the same apartment since grade school.

- Use *had* plus the past participle, usually an -*ed* ending, when you are writing in the past tense and want to refer to an earlier event.

    Ulysses S. Grant had succeeded as a general before he became president.

    After a year had passed, Margaret reconsidered her decision.

(For more on this usage, see page 51.)

FUTURE TENSES

There are three common ways to indicate the future:

> They will build their house next spring.
>
> They are going to build their house next spring.
>
> They are building their house next spring.

These three forms are nearly interchangeable.

TO VERBS (INFINITIVES)

To verbs can be used with other verbs in present, past, or future tenses. After *to,* always use the basic form of the verb with no added *-s* or *-ed.*

> To succeed in any field you need to feel passion for it.

◼ HELPING VERBS

Be verbs: *am, is, are, was, were*

Be verbs are used as helping verbs with *-ing* verbs or with past participles—usually *-ed.*

> I am driving across Canada this summer.
>
> The Statue of Liberty was presented to us by France.

Have verbs: *have, has, had*

Have verbs are used as helping verbs with past participles—usually *-ed.*

> We have followed Pat's advice quite enough.
>
> Arlene has always wanted a pig as a pet.

Other Helping Verbs

The following helping verbs are always used with the basic verb form with no -*ed*.

do	will	shall	can	may
does	would	should	could	might
did				must

As a young man, Charles could lift two hundred pounds.

They finally did clean up the river last month.

Visitors to the park must register at the rangers' office.

- *Don't, doesn't,* and *didn't* are very commonly used to negate the main verb.

We don't enjoy the beach.

Simon doesn't live in a penthouse apartment.

She didn't watch television for three months.

- *Be* and *have* sometimes can follow other helping verbs.

Their motives can be understood easily.

He should have gone to the doctor weeks ago.

◼ IRREGULAR VERBS

Most verbs form their tenses by adding *s* or *ed*. These are called *regular* verbs.

Here is the usual pattern for regular verbs:

Present	*Past*	*Past Participle* (*after* have *or* be *verbs*)
move, moves	moved	moved
talk, talks	talked	talked

In other words, today it *moves*, yesterday it *moved*, lately it *has moved* or it *was moved*.

However, a number of verbs form their tenses irregularly. On the following page is a list of twenty-five sometimes troublesome verbs. You can check your verb tenses against this list. If you don't find a verb in the list, check a dictionary. Most dictionaries list the forms of irregular verbs under the basic form.

The Most Common Irregular Verbs

Present	Past	Past Participle (after have or be verbs)
am, is, are	was, were	been
bring	brought	brought
come	came	come
cost, costs	cost	cost
do, does	did	done
draw	drew	drawn
drink	drank	drunk
eat	ate	eaten
fall	fell	fallen
fly	flew	flown
freeze	froze	frozen
get	got	gotten
go	went	gone
grow	grew	grown
have, has	had	had
know	knew	known
lay (put)	laid	laid
lie (recline)	lay	lain
rise (get up)	rose	risen
run	ran	run
see	saw	seen
shine (sparkle)	shone	shone
shrink	shrank	shrunk
speak	spoke	spoken
throw	threw	thrown

Shifting Verb Tenses

Sometimes you may find yourself slipping back and forth between present and past verb tenses. Be consistent, especially within each paragraph.

Present Tense for Literature

Use the present tense for writing about literature.

> Scarlett comes into the room and pulls down the draperies.
> Hamlet speaks with irony even about death.

Past Tense for Telling Stories

Use the simple past tense to tell your own stories or stories from history.

> On a dare, I jumped off the back of the garage.
> President Truman waved from the caboose.

Troublesome Verbs

Had

Watch out for *had:* You often don't need it. Use *had* to refer to events that were already finished when your story or example took place—the past before the past that you're describing. To check, try adding *previously* or *already* next to *had*.

> In 1986, we moved to New York. We had lived in Florida for three years.

> If I had known about tse-tse flies, I would have been much more cautious.

Would

Most of the time, you can leave out *would*. Use it for something that happened regularly during a period of the past.

> The teacher would always make us stand up when she entered the room.

Also use *would* for hypothetical situations.

> Elaine would have preferred to stay home.
>
> If Jack had called two minutes sooner, Elaine wouldn't be in Japan right now.
>
> If Jack were more responsible, he would think ahead.

(Use *were* with a singular subject after *if* or *as though*.)

Could, Can

Use *could* to refer to the past and *can* to refer to the present.

> *Past:* Frank couldn't swim in the ocean because it was too rough.
>
> *Present:* Frank can't swim in the ocean because it's too rough.

Use *could* to show what might happen and doesn't; use *can* to show ability.

> My parents make good money. They *could* buy us anything we want, but they don't.
>
> My parents make good money. They *can* buy us anything we want.

Gone, Eaten, Done, Seen, Written

Avoid expressions such as *I seen* and *He has went.* Use *gone, eaten, done, seen, written* after a helping verb.

We went.	We have gone.
I ate.	I have eaten.
He did it.	He has done it.
He saw the light.	He has seen the light.
She wrote	She has written
for an hour.	for an hour.

VERB AGREEMENT

The word before the verb is not always its subject. Look for *who* or *what* is doing the action.

- Remember that two singular subjects joined by *and* (for example, the bird and the bee) make a plural and need a plural verb.

  The bird and the bee make music together.
  My great aunt and my grandfather argue incessantly.

- Sometimes an insertion separates the subject and verb.

  The drummer, not the other musicians, sets the rhythm.
  The lady who sells flowers has a mysterious voice.

- Sometimes an *of* phrase separates the subject and verb; read the sentence without the *of* phrase.

  One of the guests was a sleepwalker.
  Each of us owns a Wurlitzer juke box.
  The use of cigarettes is dangerous.

- The subject of the sentence follows *there was, there were, there is, there are.*

  There was one cow in the entire field.
  There were two cows in the backyard.

- Words with *one* and *body* are singular.

  Everyone except for the twins was laughing.
  Somebody always overheats the copying machine.

- Sometimes a group can be singular.

  My family does not eat crowder peas.
  In some states the jury elects the foreman.
  A thousand dollars is a lot of money to carry around.

- *-ing* phrases are usually singular.

  Dating two people is tricky.

WORD ENDINGS: *S* AND *ED*

If word endings give you problems, train yourself to check every noun to see if it needs *s* and every verb to see if it needs *s* or *ed.*

Add *ed*

- To form most simple past tenses

    She walked.   He tripped.   Mae asked a question.

- After *has, have, had*

    He has walked.   We have moved.   She had already
                                                                arrived.

- After the *be* verbs (*are, were, is, was, am, be, been, being*)

    They are prejudiced against immigrants.
    She was depressed.
    Marge is engaged to be married.

Note that the *-ed* ending can sometimes appear in present and future tenses:

    They are supposed to leave on Friday.
    He will be prepared.

Do Not Add *ed*

- After *to*

    He loved to walk.

- After *would, should, could*

    Sometimes he would walk three miles.
    He should walk every day.

- After *did, didn't*

    He didn't walk very often.

- After an irregular past tense

    I bought bread.   She found her keys.
    The cup fell.   The shoes cost only seven dollars.

Add *s*

- To form a plural (more than one)

  many scientists   two potatoes   several families

- To the present tense of a verb that follows *he, she, it,* or a singular noun

  He walks four miles a day.   It appears every spring.
  She says very little.   The dog sees the fire hydrant.
  Bill asks provocative questions.   Polly insists on her rights.

Note: Usually when there is an *s* on the noun, there is no *s* on the verb.

  Pots rattle.   A pot rattles.
  The candles burn swiftly.   The candle burns swiftly.

- To form a possessive (with an apostrophe)

  John's mother   today's society
  Sally's house   women's clothing

Do Not Add *s* to a Verb

- If there is an *s* on the subject of the sentence or if there are two subjects

  Tulips come from Holland.
  Salt and sugar look the same.

- If one of these helping verbs comes before the main verb

does	may	will	shall	can
must	might	would	should	could

  Kenneth should clean out the back seat of his car.
  Angelica can get there in thirty minutes.
  The professor's attitude does make me angry.

For more help with word endings, see pages 11–12, 18, 46–50, and 53.

TANGLED SENTENCES

Look at your sentences to make sure the parts go with each other.

▨ PARALLEL STRUCTURE

The parts of a list (or pair) must be in the same format.

Not
Parallel: I love to play music, to dance, and just being with my friends.

Here, two verbs have *to,* but the last has an *-ing* ending.

Correct: I love to play music, to dance, and just to be with my friends.

Correct: I love playing music, dancing, and just being with my friends.

Not
Parallel: To reach the camp, Marty paddled a canoe and then a horse.

Here, it sounds as if Marty paddled a horse.

Correct: To reach the camp, Marty paddled a canoe and then rode a horse.

Not
Parallel: Go to the trunk and take out your tools, your jack, and don't forget your spare tire.

Here, all the parts of the list should be nouns.

Correct: Go to the trunk and take out your tools, your jack, and your spare tire.

Not
Parallel: My father has told me stories that have made me laugh, amazed me, gave me the willies, and that have taught me lessons.

Here, the helping verb *have* goes with the verbs *made, amazed,* and *taught,* but not with *gave.* In addition, *that have* is suddenly repeated near the end.

Correct: My father has told me stories that have made me laugh, amazed me, given me the willies, and taught me lessons.

◼ DANGLERS

- There are two problems. In one, a word (often a pronoun) has been left out, so that the introductory phrase doesn't fit with what follows.

Dangler: Dashing wildly across the platform, the subway pulled out of the station.

This sounds as if the subway dashed across the platform. To correct it, add the missing word or words.

Correct: Dashing wildly across the platform, we saw the subway pull out of the station.

Correct: As we dashed wildly across the platform, the subway pulled out of the station.

Dangler: At the age of five, my sister took me to school for the first time.

Technically, this sentence says that the sister was five.

Correct: When I was five, my sister took me to school for the first time.

- The second problem occurs when a phrase or word in a sentence is too far from the part it goes with.

Dangler: A former athlete, the reporters interviewed Terrence Harley about the use of steroids.

This sounds as if the reporters are a former athlete.

Correct: The reporters interviewed Terrence Harley, a former athlete, about the use of steroids.

■ MIXED SENTENCE PATTERNS

Sometimes you start with one way of getting to a point, but one of the words slides you into a different way of saying it. The two patterns get mixed up. Correct a mixed sentence by using one pattern or the other.

Mixed
(incorrect):   By opening the window lets in fresh air.

Here the writer started to say "By opening the window, I let in fresh air," but the phrase *opening the window* took over.

Correct: By opening the window, I let in fresh air.

Correct: Opening the window lets in fresh air.

Read your sentence as a whole to make sure that the end goes with the beginning.

Mixed
(incorrect):   In the Republic of Cameroon has over two hundred local languages.

Correct: The Republic of Cameroon has over two hundred local languages.

Correct: In the Republic of Cameroon, over two hundred local languages are spoken.

Mixed
(incorrect):   In "London," by William Blake presents a critique of the modern city.

Correct: In "London," William Blake presents a critique of the modern city.

Note that these problem sentences most often begin with *by* or *in*.

PART 2

PUTTING A PAPER TOGETHER

What to Do When You're Stuck
Finding an Organization for Your Essay
How to Work on a Second Draft
How to Make a Paper Longer (and When to Make It Shorter)
Introductions and Conclusions
Paragraphs—Long and Short
Transitions
Proofreading Tips

What to Do When You're Stuck

Sometimes the ideas don't seem to be there, or you have only two ideas, or your thoughts are disconnected and jumbled. Sometimes it's hard to know where to begin or what shape your writing should take.

Here are some techniques used by professional writers. Try several—some are better for particular kinds of writing. For instance, lists and outlines work when you don't have much time (in an essay exam) or when you have many points to include. Freewriting works well when your topic is subtle, when you want to write with depth. You'll find several techniques that work for you.

▣ Techniques That Work

Break the Assignment into Easy Steps

You can take an intimidating assignment one step at a time. Start where you're most comfortable. Often, once you have some ideas written, one will lead to another, and you'll have a whole draft of your paper. Otherwise, by trying several of the following techniques, you may find that your paper is partly written and you have a clear sense of how to finish it.

Freewriting

In this method, you find your ideas by writing with no plan, quickly, without stopping. Don't worry about what to say first. Start somewhere in the middle. Just write nonstop for ten to twenty minutes. Ignore grammar, spelling, organization. Follow your thoughts as they come. Above all, don't stop! If you hit a blank place, write your last word over and over—you'll soon have a new idea. After you have freewritten several times, read what you've written and underline the good sentences. These can be the heart of your essay. Freewriting takes time, but it is the easiest way to begin and leads to surprising and creative results.

Lists and Outlines

With this method, before you write any sentences, you make a list of the points you might use in your essay, including any examples and details that come to mind. Jot them down briefly, a word or phrase for each item. Keeping these points brief makes them easier to read and rearrange. Include any ideas you think of in one long list down the page. When you run dry, wait a little—more ideas will come.

Now start grouping the items on the list. Draw lines connecting examples to the points they illustrate. Then make a new list with the related points grouped together. Decide which idea is most important and cross out ideas or details that do not relate to it. Arrange your points so that each will lead up to the next. Be sure each section of your essay has examples or facts to strengthen your ideas.

You're ready to write. You'll see that this system works best when you have a big topic with many details. Although it seems complicated, it actually saves time. Once you have your plan, the writing of the essay will go very fast.

Writing a Short Draft First

In one page, write your ideas for the assignment, what you've thought of including. Take just ten or twenty minutes. Now you have a draft to work with. Expand each point with explanations or examples.

A similar technique is to write just one paragraph—at least six sentences—that tells the main ideas you have in mind. Arrange the sentences in a logical and effective sequence. Then copy each sentence from that core paragraph onto its own page and write a paragraph or two to back up each sentence. Now you have the rough draft of an essay. Remember, your first draft doesn't have to be perfect as long as it's good enough for you to work with.

Using a Tape Recorder

If you have trouble writing as fast as you think, talk your ideas into a recorder. Play them back several times, stopping to write down the best sentences. Another method is to write down four or five sentences before you begin, each starting with the main word of your topic, each different from the others. As you talk, use these sentences to get going when you run dry and to make sure you discuss different aspects of your topic.

A Relaxation Technique to Clear Your Mind

Sit up straight in a chair, put your feet flat on the floor, and place your palms on your thighs. Breathe very slowly, feeling the air spiral through your body. Focus on a spot on the floor. Feel each part of your body relax, starting with your feet. Take your time. Listen to the most distant sounds you can hear, the faintest sounds. Take several minutes or more being still, concentrating on your slow breathing. Then take a deep breath and begin to freewrite.

Talking to a Friend

The idea here is for your friend to help you discover and organize *your* ideas—not to tell you his or her ideas. The best person for this technique is not necessarily a good writer but a good listener. Ask your friend just to listen and not say anything for a few minutes. As you talk, you might jot down points you make. Then ask what came across most vividly. As your friend responds, you may find yourself saying more, trying to make a point clearer. Make notes of the new points, but don't let your friend write or dictate words for you. Once you have plenty of notes, you're ready to be alone and to freewrite or outline.

■ TIME WASTERS: WHAT *NOT* TO DO

Don't Recopy Repeatedly

Get down a complete first draft before you try to revise any of it. You might write on every second or third line so that you can revise easily. Keep a sheet of note paper handy to jot down new thoughts when they occur, and place a number or star to mark the places where you plan to insert new thoughts.

Don't Use a Dictionary or Thesaurus before the Second Draft

Delay your concern for precise word usage and spelling until you have the whole paper written. Then go back and make improvements.

Don't Spend Hours on an Outline

You will probably revise your outline after the first draft, so don't get bogged down at the beginning. Even with long papers, a topic outline (naming the idea for each paragraph without supporting details) is often an efficient way to organize.

If you use notecards, arrange them according to the paragraph topics they support, rather than copying them onto an outline.

Don't Try to Make Only One Draft

You may think you can save time by writing only one draft, but you can't get everything perfect the first time. Actually, it's faster to write something *approximately* close to the points you want to make, then go back and revise.

Don't Write with Distractions

When you write, you need to focus your physical and mental energy. You can be distracted by music, television, or conversation in the background or by being too uncomfortable or too comfortable. You may not even realize how much these distractions can diffuse your energy and concentration.

Finding an Organization for Your Essay

Your goal in organizing is to produce a sequence of paragraphs that leads the reader to a single strong conclusion. But there are many ways to reach this goal.

Some people need an outline; others write first and then reorganize when they see a pattern in their writing. Still others begin in the middle or write the parts of their papers out of order.

No method is the "right" one. Some approaches are better for certain topics; some are better for certain people. Do not feel that you have to fit into a set way of working.

Using a Formula as a Plan

Sometimes a teacher will give you a specific format to follow, but most of the time you will need to discover the organization that best enhances the content of your essay. A formula is especially useful for assignments you must do repeatedly or quickly. For instance, lab reports usually follow a set format: (1) Question to be Investigated; (2) The Experiment; (3) Observations; (4) Conclusions. Some topics lend themselves to particular arrangements. Here are a few:

Common Patterns of Organization

chronological (the sequence in which events occurred)
narrative (how you learned what you know)
generalization, followed by examples or arguments
process (the steps for how something is done)
comparison (similarities and differences)
classification (types and categories)
problem and solution
cause and effect
a brief case study or story, followed by interpretation of what it shows
dramatic order (building to the strongest point)

If what you want to say fits one of these patterns, you can organize your paper efficiently. However, formulas quite often create boring papers. For most topics you will need to discover the best plan by making lists of ideas and reordering them, or by writing for a while and then reworking what you've written.

Creating a Rough Outline

Here's a method that works for many writers:

- Make a random list—written in *phrases*, not sentences—of all the ideas and facts you want to include. Don't be stingy. Make a long list.

- Now look at your list and decide which are your main points and which points support them.

- Write a single sentence or two that contain the major point you are going to make. Make sure that this point is stated early in your essay.

- Decide on the order of your main points.

- Cross off points from your list that do not fit the pattern or plan you are using. Remember, you can't put in everything you know.

- Decide on your paragraphs; write a sentence for each paragraph that tells what you plan to say.

- Now start writing. Get a rough draft finished before you reconsider your organization.

When to Adjust Your Plan

Sometimes the trick to good organization is *reorganization*. No matter whether you start with an outline, no matter what you think when you begin, your topic may well shift and change as you write. Often you will come up with better ideas, and as a result, you may change your emphasis. Therefore, you must be ready to abandon parts or all of your original plan. Some minor points may now become major points. Most writers need to revise their plan *after* they finish a first draft.

Here are the signs that a paper needs to be reorganized:

- Parts of the paper are boring.

- Your real point doesn't show up until the end.

- You have repeated the same idea in several different places.

- The essay seems choppy and hard to follow.

- Your paragraphs are either too short or too long.

In the end, make sure that you know the main point you want the reader to get and that every sentence contributes to making that point clear.

How to Work on a Second Draft

Revision is not just fixing errors. It means taking a fresh look at all aspects of your paper, moving some parts of it, and completely rewriting others. Look at your first draft from the following angles.

The Real Goal of Your Paper

- A big danger is straying from your subject. It's tempting to include good ideas or long examples that are related to your subject but do not support your main point.

- You might find it helpful to write a sentence that begins, "The main point of my paper is. . . ." This sentence should not go into your paper, but keep it in front of you as you revise to make sure that every detail supports your main point. Notice that your *real* point may not be the point with which you started. As you look over your work, decide what you are really saying. You may need to write a new introduction that stresses your real goal.

The Order of Your Points

If you have trouble getting from one point to the next, you may need to omit one point or move your points around.

- Make a list of your points in the order you wrote them.
- Now play with the order so that each one logically leads to the next.
- Get rid of points that aren't related.
- Cover some points briefly as parts of other points.

Strong Parts and Weak Parts

- Build up what's good. When revising, writers tend to focus on the weak spots. Instead, start by looking for the good parts in your paper. Underline or highlight them, and write more about them. Add examples. Explain more fully. You may find that you have written a new, much better paper.

- Fix up what's bad. Now look at the parts that are giving you trouble. Do you really need them? Are they in the right place? If you got tangled up trying to say something that you consider important, stop and ask yourself, "What is it I'm trying to say, after all?" Then say it to yourself in plain English and write it down that way.

Reading Aloud to a Friend

- When you read your paper to a friend, notice what you *add* as you read—what information or explanations you feel compelled to put in. Jot down these additions and put them into the paper.

- Ask your friend to tell you what came through. All you want is what he or she heard—not whether it's good, not how to change it. Then let your friend ask you questions. However, don't let your friend take over and tell you what to write.

Final Touches

- Look again at the proportions of your paper. Are some of the paragraphs too short and choppy? Is there one that is overly long?

- Look at your introduction and conclusion. You may find that your old first paragraph is no longer your real point. If so, write a new one. Play with the first and last sentences of your paper in order to begin and end with the strongest statements that you can. Write the idea three or four different ways—with very different wording—then choose the best.

- Write a title that catches the reader's attention and announces your specific subject.

- Proofread your paper closely several times and make corrections. Watch especially for errors in any of the new material you've written. If you revise on a computer, be sure to use the spellcheck to catch trouble spots and, after you print your paper, proofread the hard copy.

How to Make a Paper Longer (and When to Make It Shorter)

Adding words and phrases to your paper makes it at most an inch longer. Adding new points or new examples will make it grow half a page at a time. On the other hand, there are times when cutting a little bit will make your whole paper stronger.

How to Make a Paper Longer

- Add an example or explain your reasons to clarify your point—or even add a new point.

- Mention other views of the subject that differ from yours: either incorporate them (showing the evidence for them) or disprove them (telling why others might accept them and why you reject them).

- Add details (facts, events that happened, things you can see or hear). Details are the life of a paper. Instead of writing, "We got something to drink," write "We took water from the stream with Stacey's tin cup. The water was so cold it hurt our stomachs."

- Expand your conclusion: Discuss implications and questions that your paper brings to mind.

but

- Don't add empty phrases, because they make your writing boring. Don't fake length by using fat margins, big handwriting, or a large typeface.

When to Make a Paper Shorter

- Condense minor points. Sometimes you think a point is necessary, but when you read your paper to a friend, you notice that you both get bored in that section. Or sometimes you get tangled up trying to make a point clear when you can cover it briefly or cut it entirely.

- Watch your *pace* when you tell a series of events. Head toward the main point or event directly. Don't get lost in boring preliminary details.

- Avoid getting sidetracked. The digression may interest you, but it may not add to the real point of the essay.

- Check to see if you have repeated any point several times. If so, decide on the most effective place to make that point and make it fully in one place.

Introductions and Conclusions

Beginnings and endings of everything, including written essays, demand special attention. After you've written your paper, pretend that you are a reader leafing through a magazine. Would you stop to read your paper? Would you lose interest at the end? You may need to add an introduction that snags a reader's interest or a conclusion that puts what you've written into perspective.

To get a memorable first or last sentence, try writing *five* sentences. They can express the same basic idea, but they should be worded as differently as possible—one long, one short, one plain, one elegant. If you write five, you'll find the one you want.

☐ Introductions

In an essay exam or under time pressure, write the introduction first to indicate the map of the paper. Sometimes you may get stuck writing an introduction. In that case, try writing your introduction *after* you've written the rest of the first draft. Often you don't find your real main point until you've written several pages.

Here are a few common methods for beginning an essay:

Indicate the Parts of Your Essay

In many academic papers and in technical or business reports, the introduction should indicate what is coming. Write a brief paragraph summing up the points you plan to make, one at a time. Then, in the middle of your paper, develop each point into a paragraph.

> There were three causes of the sudden population increase in eighteenth-century Europe. First, the newly settled colonies provided enough wealth to support more people. Second, eighteenth-century wars did not kill as many Europeans as did seventeenth-century wars. Finally, the discovery of the potato provided a cheap food source.

Sometimes you can indicate the parts of your essay more subtly:

> Although *Walden* and *Adventures of Huckleberry Finn* treat similar themes, the two books have very different tones and implications.

Take a Bold Stand

Start out with a strong statement of your position.

> Millard Filmore is the most underrated President in American history.

Start with the Other Side

Tell what you disagree with and who said it. Give the opposing reasons so that you can later prove them wrong. For examples of this technique, see the editorial or "opinion" page of your newspaper.

Tell a Brief Story

Give one or two paragraphs to a single typical case, and then make your general point. The brief story makes clear the personal implications of the topic you will present.

Move from the General to the Specific

Begin with the wider context of the topic and then zero in on the case at hand.

> When we think of "strength," we usually picture physical strength–for instance, a weight lifter. But there are subtler forms of strength. Perhaps the rarest is moral strength: the ability to do what is right, even when it is inconvenient, unpopular, or dangerous. My grandfather in Italy was actually a strongman in the circus, but I remember him for his moral strength rather than for his powerful arms.

Use the News Lead

Write one sentence incorporating *who, what, when, where, how,* and sometimes *why.*

> During the fourteenth century, in less than three years, one-third of Europe's population died of the bubonic plague.

◻ CONCLUSIONS

Don't end your paper with preaching or clichés. Consider, out of all that you have written, what is most important. Sometimes you want a quick summation, but other times you will have a longer conclusion that probes your topic more deeply.

Here are several approaches to writing a conclusion:

Summarize

Stress your main points, but avoid repeating earlier phrases word for word.

Suggest a Solution to a Problem

Come up with a solution you think might make a difference, and tell how the information you've presented could affect the future.

Put Your Ideas in a Wider Perspective

What is the importance of what you have said? What is the larger meaning? Move from the specifics of your topic to the deeper concerns it suggests.

Raise Further Questions or Implications

Which issues now remain? Acknowledge the limitations of what you have covered. Reaffirm what you *have* established. Examine what it implies.

Paragraphs— Long and Short

The paragraphs of your essay lead the reader step by step through your ideas. Each paragraph should make one point, and every sentence in it should relate to that one point. Usually the paragraph begins by stating the point and then goes on to explain it and make it specific.

Paragraphs should be as long as they need to be to make one point. Sometimes one or two strong sentences can be enough. At other times you need nine or ten sentences to explain your point. However, you want to avoid writing an essay that consists of either one long paragraph or a series of very short ones. Paragraphs give readers a visual landing, a place to pause; so use your eye and vary the lengths of your paragraphs.

◼ Indent the First Word of the Paragraph

In college papers, indent the first word of each paragraph *five* spaces in typing, and approximately that amount of space if you are writing by hand. In business letters or reports, where you single-space between lines, omit the indentation and double-space between the paragraphs to divide them.

◼ Break Up Long Paragraphs

A paragraph that is more than ten sentences usually should be divided. Find a natural point for division, such as

- A new subject or idea

- A turning point in a story

- The start of an example

- A change of location or time

■ EXPAND SHORT PARAGRAPHS

Too many short paragraphs can make your thought seem fragmented. If you have a string of paragraphs that consist of one or two sentences, you may need to *combine, develop,* or *omit* some of your paragraphs.

Combine

- Join two paragraphs on the same point.
- Include examples in the same paragraph as the point they illustrate.
- Regroup your major ideas and make a new paragraph plan.

Develop

- Give examples or reasons to support your point.
- Cite facts, statistics, or evidence to support your point.
- Relate an incident or event that supports your point.
- Explain any important general terms.
- Quote authorities to back up what you say.

Omit

If you have a short paragraph that cannot be expanded or combined with another, chances are that paragraph should be dropped. Sometimes you have to decide whether you really want to explain a particular point or whether it's not important to your paper.

■ CHECK FOR CONTINUITY

Within a paragraph, make sure that your sentences follow a logical sequence. Each one should build on the previous one and lead to the next.

Link your paragraphs together with transitions—taking words or ideas from one paragraph and using them at the beginning of the next one.

☐ A TIP

If you keep having trouble with your paragraphs, you can rely on this basic paragraph pattern:

- A main point stated in one sentence
- An explanation of any general words in your main point
- Examples or details that support your point
- The reason each example supports your point
- A sentence to sum up

TRANSITIONS

Transitions are *bridges* in your writing that take the reader from one thought to the next. These bridges link your ideas and help you to avoid choppy writing. You need transitions between paragraphs that show the movement from one idea to the next, and you also need transitions to connect sentences within a paragraph.

First Check the Order of Your Ideas

If you are having trouble with transitions, it may be that your points are out of order. Make a list of your points and juggle the order so that one point leads logically to the next. Then add transitions that underscore the movement from one point to the other.

Use Transition Words

Keep your transitions brief and inconspicuous. Here are some choices of transition words you can use to illustrate certain points or relationships:

Adding a point:	furthermore, besides, finally, in addition to
Emphasis:	above all, indeed, in fact, in other words, most important
Time:	then, afterwards, eventually, next, immediately, meanwhile, previously, already, often, since then, now, later, usually
Space:	next to, across, from, above, below, nearby, inside, beyond, between, surrounding
Cause and effect:	consequently, as a result, therefore, thus
Examples:	for example, for instance
Progression:	first, second, third, furthermore

Contrast:	but, however, in contrast, instead, nevertheless, on the other hand, though, still, unfortunately
Similarity:	like, also, likewise, similarly, as, then too
Concession:	although, yet, of course, after all, granted, while it is true
Conclusions:	therefore, to sum up, in brief, in general, in short, for these reasons, in retrospect, finally, in conclusion

Use Repetition of Key Words

- Repeat the word itself or variations of it.

  I can never forget the *year* of the flood. That was the *year* I grew up.

  Everyone agreed that Adlai Stevenson was *intelligent.* His *intelligence,* however, did not always endear him to the voters.

- Use pronouns.

  People who have hypoglycemia usually need to be on a special diet. *They* should, at the very least, avoid eating sugar.

- Use synonyms—different words with the same meaning.

  When you repot plants, be certain to use a high grade of potting *soil.* Plants need good rich *dirt* in order to thrive.

  Even though the woman was *handcuffed,* she kept running around, waving her *manacled* hands in the air.

Use Transitional Sentences to Link Paragraphs

Usually the transition between paragraphs comes in the first sentence of the new paragraph.

  Even though Hortense followed all of these useful suggestions, she still ran into an unforeseen problem.

  Because of these results, the researchers decided to try a new experiment.

Notice that, in these examples, the first half of the sentence refers to a previous paragraph; the second half points to the paragraph that is beginning.

Proofreading Tips

The key to proofreading is doing it several times. Careless errors undermine what you have said, so make a practice of proofreading methodically.

Here are some tips to help you spot mistakes.

Make a Break between Writing and Proofreading

Always put a little distance between the writing of a paper and the proofreading of it. That way you'll see it fresh and catch errors you might have otherwise overlooked. Set the paper aside for the night—or even for twenty minutes—while you catch your breath. When you write in class, train yourself *not* to write up until the final moment; give yourself an extra ten minutes before the end of class, take a short break, and then proofread your paper several times before handing it in.

Search for Trouble

Assume that you have made unconscious errors and really look for them. Slow down your reading considerably, and actually look at every word.

Know Your Own Typical Mistakes

Before you proofread, look over any papers you've already gotten back corrected. Recall the errors you need to watch for. As you're writing *this* paper, take ten minutes to learn from the last one.

Proofread for One Type of Error

If periods and commas are your biggest problem, or if you always leave off apostrophes, or if you always write *your* for *you're*, go through the paper checking for just that one problem. Then go back and proofread to check for other mistakes.

Proofread Out of Order

Try starting with the last sentence of the paper and reading backwards to the first sentence; or proofread the second half of the paper first (since that's where most of the errors usually are), take a break, and then proofread the first half.

Proofread Aloud

Try always to read your paper aloud at least once. This will slow you down, and you'll *hear* the difference between what you meant to write and what you actually wrote.

Look Up Anything You're Not Sure Of

Use this book and a dictionary. You'll learn nothing by guessing, but you'll learn something forever if you take the time to look it up.

Proofread Your Final Copy Several Times

It does no good to proofread a draft of your paper and then forget to proofread the final copy. This problem crops up often, especially in typewritten papers. Remember: A *typo* is just as much an error as any other error.

With a Computer, Proofread on Both Screen and Page

If you are using a computer, scroll through and make corrections on the screen. Double-check places where you have inserted or deleted material. Use the spellcheck, but remember that it will not catch commonly confused words like *to* and *too* or *your* and *you're*.

PART 3

MEETING SPECIFIC ASSIGNMENTS

Format of College Papers
Writing in Class
Writing About Literature
How to Quote from Your Sources
Using the College Library and the Internet
Writing Research Papers
Plagiarism (Cheating)
Documentation

FORMAT OF COLLEGE PAPERS

■ TYPING YOUR PAPER

Paper

- Use 8½″ × 11″ white paper.
- If you use computer paper, separate the pages and remove the perforated edges.
- Staple once or clip in the upper left-hand corner.

Typeface

- If you have a choice, use a 12 point serif typeface on the computer.
- Do not use all capital letters or all italics.

Spacing

- Double-space between lines; you should get approximately twenty-seven lines per page. (Double-space even for long quotations.)
- Use an inch to an inch-and-a-half margin on all four sides.
- Indicate the beginning of each paragraph either by indenting the first line five spaces or by skipping a line and starting at the left margin (block format). Do not mix these methods.
- Do not justify (line up the margin) on the right unless asked to do so. Justifying on the right distorts the spacing between letters and words, making your paper harder to read.
- At the bottom of the page, use a full last line, unless you're ending a paragraph. It's all right to end a page in mid-sentence.

Spacing After Punctuation

- Leave *two* spaces after

  Periods   Question marks   Exclamation marks

  Note: The MLA (Modern Language Association) now permits one space after a period, question mark, or exclamation mark.

- Leave *one* space after

  Commas   Colons   Semicolons

- Make a dash by using two hyphens—with no space before or after.

- Make an ellipsis (. . .) by using three periods with a space before and after each period.

- Never begin a line with a period or a comma.

- Never put a space before a punctuation mark (except for an ellipsis or an opening parenthesis).

Dividing Words

- Avoid, as much as possible, dividing a word from one line to the next. If you can, fit it on one line or the other.

- If you must divide a very long word, divide only between syllables. To find the syllables, look up the word in a dictionary. It will be printed with dots between the syllables: *ex • per • i • men • ta • tion.*

- Never divide a one-syllable word, like *brought.* Never divide a word after only one letter.

Page Numbers

Put your last name and page number on each page after the first.

Cover Sheet or First Page

Include:

- The title, without quotation marks or underlining
- Your name

- The course title and number
- The teacher's name
- The date

If you use a cover sheet, center the title in the middle of the page, and put the other information in the lower right-hand corner. If you don't use a cover sheet, put your name, etc., in the upper-left corner; then skip two lines and center the title.

◼ SUBMITTING PAPERS ELECTRONICALLY

When you submit a paper electronically, save it as a text file, skip a line between paragraphs, and number your paragraphs (putting the numbers in brackets). Use one underline before and after a title you normally would underline.

◼ A WORD ABOUT PROOFREADING

No matter who has typed your paper, you must read the typed copy several times. A typo counts as an error; it's no excuse to say, "Oh, that's just a typo." (If a friend or relative does type for you, be sure that the typist doesn't interfere with the content. Don't let someone else tell you how to do your assignment.)

Often teachers don't mind if you correct your typed copy with a pen. If it's okay with your teacher, you can draw a line through the word you wish to change and write the correction above the line. Small corrections can also be made with correction fluid. If you use a computer, proofread your paper both on the monitor and on the printout. Don't rely solely on a spellcheck; it will miss errors like *to* for *too*.

Writing in Class

A wave of panic—that's what most people feel when they are handed an assignment to be written in class. Some students, feeling the pressure, plunge in and write the first thoughts that come to mind. But your first thoughts aren't necessarily your best thoughts. There's a smarter way to write in a limited time.

Take Your Time at the Beginning

- Re-read the instructions carefully. Be sure you're writing what you've been asked for.

- Jot down brief notes for a few minutes. Don't write whole sentences yet—just a word or phrase for each idea, example, or fact.

- Take a few more minutes to expand your notes. Stay calm. Don't start writing too soon.

- Decide on the parts of your essay.

For an Essay About Information, Stress Your Organization

- Write an introduction that indicates the parts of your essay. One simple technique is to give a full sentence in your introduction for each of the main points you plan to make:

  > Sigmund Freud is famous for three important ideas. He popularized the idea that we repress or bottle up our feelings. He explored the idea of the unconscious. Most important, he stressed the idea that our family relationships when we are children determine our adult relationships.

Note how the number "three" in the first sentence helps the reader to see the plan of the whole essay.

- Write a paragraph for each point using the same order as you did in your introduction. In each middle paragraph, restate the point, explain what you mean by any general words, and give facts or examples to prove your point.

- Write a brief conclusion, stressing what's most important.

- For *short essays on an exam,* each answer should consist of one long paragraph. Write a one-sentence introduction that uses words from the question and asserts your answer. Then, in the same paragraph, present three facts to support your answer, explaining one fact at a time. Finally, sum up your position in the last sentence of the paragraph.

For a Personal Essay, Stress What You Have Discovered

While the three-point essay can get you by, it can easily become stilted and boring. In a personal essay, you have many more options.

- If you're asked to write about a significant event in your life, begin your essay by describing it *briefly.* Use vivid details to bring it to life. Then use most of your essay to tell what you learned from this event or how it has changed you. Remember to divide your essay into paragraphs.

- If you're asked to give your opinion about a topic, you sometimes can use personal examples to support your position. In your introduction make clear where you stand. Then give each important point its own paragraph with examples. Use your own experiences, your own observations, and incidents you've read about.

- If you can't come up with a strong introduction at first, go ahead and write your essay. In the process you might discover a central idea that can then serve as your introduction.

- In your conclusion, don't preach and don't fall back on overused generalizations. Say what matters to you or what you have discovered.

Here are some other tips to save time:

Don't Start Over

- Stick to your plan. If you get a new idea, use an asterisk (*) or an arrow to show where it goes.

- Leave room after each paragraph for ideas you might want to add later. If you are writing in an exam booklet, write on only the front side of the page so that you will have room for insertions.

- If you add or cut a main point, go back and revise your introduction to match the change.

Don't Pad Your Writing

Use a direct, no-nonsense style. Don't try for big words—they just lead to errors when you are under time pressure. Simply state your points and the facts to back them up, one step at a time.

Don't Make a Neat Copy

Copying over wastes precious time, and the copy tends to be full of slips and errors. Instead, put a line through an error and correct it above the line; use a carat (^) for a short insertion, an asterisk (*) or arrow for a long insertion.

Don't Rush at the End

- Stop writing ten minutes before the end of the allotted time.

- Read your essay for content. Don't add to it unless you find a *major* omission. Late additions usually create errors and disorganization.

- Proofread, with special attention to the second half of the essay (where rushing leads to errors) and to the very first sentence. Look closely for the errors you usually make. Look for words like *to* and *too, then* and *than.* Check your *periods* to be sure you have no run-on sentences or fragments. Look carefully to make sure that you haven't left out any words or letters.

Writing About Literature

☐ How to Think Through Your Essay

When you are asked to write about literature, you will need to be certain of your teacher's expectations. Some teachers want a *summary* of your reading, in which you tell the main points of what you've read, followed by your evaluation. However, most literature teachers want you to stress an important idea about the reading and to demonstrate the details that gave you your idea.

Omit Plot Summary and the Author's Life

Unless you've been asked to, do not include a detailed plot summary repeating all the events of the story. Remember, the teacher already knows what the book says but does not know your ideas about the assignment. Your job is to show the reader your point about the story, rather than to tell the story. However, you will refer to details from the plot when you give examples to support your ideas.

Do not include a summary of the author's life in your essay unless you have been asked to do so.

Gather Your First Impressions of the Topic

Begin by freewriting about the question you have been asked or the topic you are considering: Write your first impressions quickly, without pausing, to get your ideas on paper. Do not worry about organization yet; don't even stop to re-read. After ten minutes, read your ideas, underline the most important, and write a sentence to sum up your main idea.

Re-Read the Text

Search for evidence to support your main idea and also for evidence that might lead you to modify it. The evidence could include incidents in a story or subtleties of style. Make notes as you re-read, and mark passages you may wish to quote.

Organize Your Essay

Do not merely follow the order of what you read. Look at your original freewriting, and revise your main idea if necessary. Decide on the parts of your idea and the order that will make them clear.

Use Evidence to Back Up Your Points

For each main point, explain which details from the reading gave you that idea. In some cases, *briefly* quote the author. After referring to a detail or quoting a passage, always explain why that detail or passage supports your point.

Write a Title for Your Paper

The title should express the main idea of your paper, not just give the title of the text.

> The Uses of Rhyme in Robert Browning's "My Last Duchess"

◼ TECHNICALITIES

Titles

<u>Underline</u> or *italicize* titles of books, periodicals, plays, films, and television programs. Put "quotation marks" around titles of stories, poems, essays, and one-act plays.

For detailed instructions about titles, see page 45.

Authors

Use the author's full name the first time you mention it. Thereafter, use the full name or last name—not the first name by itself.

> Emily Dickinson wrote 1,775 poems.

> or

> Dickinson wrote 1,775 poems.

Identifying the Title and Author

Be sure to identify the title and author early in your essay, even if you've already done so in your title.

> In "Because I Could Not Stop for Death," Emily Dickinson takes us from "immortality" to "eternity."
>
> In <u>King Lear</u>, Shakespeare examines a king's assumptions about language.
>
> "A Rose for Emily," by William Faulkner, is a study of changing social classes.
>
> <u>Anna Karenina</u>, by Leo Tolstoy, compares three marriages.

You can use this type of sentence to begin your essay, or you can introduce the general topic (death, language, social classes, marriage) and then identify the specific text you will examine.

Note carefully the punctuation in these examples. Remember that a comma or period goes inside quotation marks.

Using Correct Literary Terms

A *story* is a series of events leading to a climax. You may be writing about a story, but you are writing an essay. A *novel* is a book-length story.

Articles and *essays* are short works of nonfiction. In some cases these terms may be used interchangeably; in general, however, articles are written for publication and usually present information, while essays may or may not be written for publication and usually present reflections and ideas based upon observation.

A *poem* is arranged with *lines* of varying length; some poems are also divided into *stanzas* (groups of lines).

A *play* is a story written to be presented in a theatre. It consists mostly of the dialogue of the characters but also contains brief stage directions to describe the set, sound, costumes, and lighting and to indicate actions of the characters.

Verb Tense

Use present tense to refer to the action in a work of literature:

> The speaker of the poem longs for his youth. Early in the novel, Elizabeth misjudges Darcy.

Crediting Your Source

- If you are quoting from only one source, give information at the end of the paper on the edition you used. List the author, the title, the city of publication, the publisher, and the copyright date. If you want to provide the original date of publication, put it immediately after the title.

  > Fitzgerald, Zelda. *Save Me the Waltz.* 1960. New York: NAL, 1982.

- Directly after each quotation, give the page number in parentheses.

  > The novel ends with a couple "watching the twilight" (203).

- For a poem (such as Coleridge's "The Rime of the Ancient Mariner"), give the line numbers.

  > Water, water, every where,
  > And all the boards did shrink;
  > Water, water, every where,
  > Nor any drop to drink. (119–122)

- For the Bible, give the abbreviated title of the specific book, with chapter and verse.

  > To every thing there is a season, and a time to every purpose under the heaven. (Eccles. 3.1)

- For a play (such as Shakespeare's *Antony and Cleopatra*), give act, scene, and lines.

  > Age cannot wither her, nor custom stale
  > Her infinite variety. (2.2.234–235)

- For more than one source, see "Documentation," pages 112–125.

How to Quote from Your Sources

A good quotation demonstrates the point you are making.

Keep the Quotations Secondary to Your Own Ideas and Words

Each quotation should illustrate a definite point you want to make. Before and after the quotation, stress your point. Maintain your own writing style throughout the paper.

Don't Use Many Quotations

Too many quotations chop up your paper and lead the reader away from your points. Most of the time, tell in your own style what you found out. Instead of quoting, you can *summarize* (give the main points of what you read) or *paraphrase* (explain a single point in detail in your own words).

Keep Your Quotations Brief

Short quotations are the easiest and most graceful to use. Avoid using many quotations of over three or four lines. If you want to use a long quotation, omit sections that do not apply and use an ellipsis (. . .) to indicate the part you've left out. A long quotation should be followed by a discussion, in the same paragraph, of the points you are making about the quotation.

Introduce Your Quotations

Direct quotations should usually be preceded by identifying tags. Always make clear who is speaking and the source of the information.

> John Holt, in his essay "How Teachers Make Children Hate Reading," says, "Many children associate books and reading with mistakes."

Incorporating the author's name and any other pertinent information into your text will vary your quotations.

> Educator John Holt offers advice for how to read: "Find something, dive into it, take the good parts, skip the bad parts, get what you can out of it, go on to something else."

In any case, don't begin a sentence or a paragraph with a direct quotation without an introduction.

Incorporate Each Quotation into a Clear Sentence

Be certain that your quotations make sense, both in sentence structure and in content. If you use fragments of quotations, be certain that they are woven into complete sentences.

> John Holt believes that reading should be "an exciting, joyous adventure."

Note that the three examples in this chapter illustrate three ways to lead into and punctuate a quotation.

Here is the source for the quotations in this chapter:

> Holt, John. "How Teachers Make Children Hate Reading." *Redbook.* Nov. 1967: 50+. Rpt. in *Responding Voices.* Ed. Jon Ford and Elaine Hughes. New York: McGraw, 1997. 43–47.

Using the College Library and the Internet

There are many ways to get information. Besides reading books and articles, you also can get information through friends and interviews, through television and radio, through computers and the Internet. But the library is still your best single source of information. The danger with all of these sources is not knowing what you want and getting lost in the maze of research.

☐ Before You Plunge in

To avoid getting lost, spend some time thinking about what you want before you start. Here are three crucial preliminary steps:

- Get some background information in a textbook, an encyclopedia, or another reference book. Look for terms and authorities that are mentioned repeatedly.

- Write down the questions you hope to answer.

- Keep a list of subtopics that you can use as search terms in your research.

☐ How to Use Search Terms

Search terms are words and phrases that you can use to find materials on your topic. For example, information on pizza can be found with the search terms

fast food	*Italian cookery*	*pizza*
mozzarella	*Domino's*	*Pizza Hut*

You will need a list of search terms whether you are using the Internet, a library catalog, a computerized database, or a printed index.

Single Search Terms

You can look under only one term at a time in print and in some computerized databases; therefore, you will need to try several of your search terms when you look through each index, noting any cross references your sources provide.

Combining Search Terms

In many electronic formats, you can and should use combinations of different search terms. Let's say you're interested in the nutritional value of pizza. You can combine the general pizza terms with *nutrition, health, calories,* and *fat.* You might type in:

> *pizza and nutrition* *Domino's and fat*
> *fast food and health* *mozzarella and calories*

As you narrow the focus of your research, use narrower combinations of terms (such as *low-fat* and *pizza*) to get material that is more specific to your topic.

Searching through Menus

Often during electronic searches you will see a list of topics; click on one and you will see a list of subtopics; click on one and you'll see sub-subtopics, and so forth. This method is good for a start, but it is not as precise as combining search terms.

In your search, remember to:

- Narrow down the subject several times.

- Use synonyms for different search terms.

- Get help from the librarian or the computer helpline.

- Write down the author, title, date, and page number or Internet address each time you find information.

■ Choosing the Best Sources of Information

Search first for information electronically when you can. In the library use the computerized catalog to find books and media materials on your subject. Use the CD-ROM indexes to find articles in periodicals (journals, magazines, and newspapers). Ask the librarian for specialized databases in your subject field. On the Internet, use several different search engines and various combinations of your search terms. Be prepared to be both persistent and patient.

All books and articles are not equal. Some are too old or too specialized or too superficial for your purposes. Others are not really relevant to your specific angle on the topic. Be prepared to reject sources that don't fit your topic. Look for a mix of books and articles, making sure that most of your sources are up to date, especially for scientific and technical topics. (For literary and historical topics, some older books may be more helpful.)

Consider the level of information you require. A twenty-page paper needs much more detailed information and analysis than a five-page paper. A paper on mercury poisoning of fish will be much more complex for a class in advanced marine biology than for English 101.

☐ Finding a Book

Most libraries have their catalogs on a computer and no longer keep the public-access card catalog up to date; therefore, use the computerized catalog wherever possible. Copy down the catalog numbers you need, or have the computer print a list for you. You need the complete call number in order to locate a book. It also helps to copy down the author and title.

Books, media holdings, and reference materials are cataloged by author, title, and subject. At least in the beginning, you will be using the subject catalog to locate books and authors. On the computer, follow the system's instructions to see a "brief display," listing several books, or to see a "full display," giving detailed information about each book. Use a variety of general search terms. For example, you probably won't find a book entitled *The Nutritional Value of Pizza*, but you will find books including both of the subjects—*pizza* and *nutrition*. However, don't depend on books alone. The most current information will be found in articles.

■ Finding an Article

Reference Section

Articles in encyclopedias and specialized reference books are often the best place to start your research. The reference section of the library also contains dictionaries, bibliographies, and special collections of statistical information. You should ask the librarian where to browse for your particular subject.

Periodical Indexes and Databases

To find articles in newspapers, magazines, and journals, you will need to consult databases (on computers) and indexes (in bound volumes). *The Reader's Guide* and *The Magazine Index Plus* list all subjects covered in popular magazines. *The New York Times Index* and *The National Newspaper Index* list subjects covered in newspapers each year. In addition, nearly every subject field has its own specialized indexes and databases; ask the librarian for help.

Make a list of the periodicals and pages you want, including the date. You may need to check the *holdings file*, the list of periodicals your library carries. Sometimes you can read articles right on the computer screen. Otherwise the article will be available in a bound volume, in a loose copy, or on microfilm.

■ Finding Information on the Internet

The *Internet* is the name given to the network of all the computers in the world that can communicate with each other. Some of the computers on the Internet contain huge storehouses of information organized for easy public retrieval. Most of the information is free. Give yourself some time to explore the many different avenues of resources the Internet offers.

AVENUES OF INFORMATION

The World Wide Web (WWW) is composed of Websites that you can reach by typing in the Internet address or, with one click or keystroke, jumping from one topic or location to another.

Search engines such as *Altavista* and *Yahoo* allow you to search through lists of subtopics or to type in a combination of search terms. These will lead you to Websites. You will probably have several search engines listed when you access the Internet. Be sure to use several different search engines.

CARL (Colorado Alliance of Research Libraries) is a service that lists scholarly articles according to subject. You can order copies of the articles for a fee, or you can record the bibliographic information and find the article in your own college library. To reach CARL, type in *www.carl.org/carlweb/*

Dejanews has indexed according to topic the public conversations on Internet bulletin boards and newsgroups. You'll find a wide range of quality from commercial junk to expert opinion. To reach Dejanews, type in *www.dejanews.com*

Research libraries such as the Library of Congress and the New York Public Library have Websites that you can consult—giving you the opportunity to look at major listings of books and in some cases databases as well. Use a search engine to find a specific library, or check the comprehensive list at *www.library.usask.ca/hywebcat/*

Homepages of colleges and universities can link you to libraries and course materials developed by college faculty: reading lists, syllabuses, and so forth. You can find these homepages through search engines. Try using the name of a particular college or your topic phrase plus "college."

Government agencies and nonprofit organizations provide valuable statistics and other information through their Websites. Use a search engine and add "government" to your search terms. Look for Websites with *.gov* or *.org* in their addresses.

CAUTIONS

The Internet can take up all of your research time. If you're not careful, you can get lost—adding too many subtopics or switching to new topics until your project loses its shape and you've run out of time. Researching electronically can become a mesmerizing activity, and you might find that at the end of a pleasant afternoon there is nothing to report. Allow a limited time —thirty to sixty minutes— just to follow the links from different Websites that interest you.

The Internet is not a substitute for reading. Be sure you balance your Internet articles with books and periodicals. Many subjects are absent or treated carelessly on the Internet.

There is a lot of junk on the Internet. Although there are many legitimate Websites from government agencies and well-known sources such as the *New York Times* and the Public Broadcasting System, the quality and accuracy of statements on the Internet vary widely. No one checks or credits the information in chat rooms and most bulletin boards.

Websites are not like video games. They don't necessarily progress to higher and higher levels. A good source might lead you to a superficial source.

You may never be able to return to some sources you come across. Be methodical about using "bookmarks" if your system allows them; otherwise write down each Internet address with the title of the article.

WHEN YOU FIND TOO LITTLE OR TOO MUCH INFORMATION

The most common problems that students experience when using computerized listings are that they can't find any sources or that they find too many sources. In either case, first consult the helpline for the particular listings.

No Match for Your Request

- You may have misspelled one or more words.

- You may have used the wrong symbols or phrasing for that particular search engine.

- You may have submitted too narrow a search. Try generalizing a bit—for example change the phrase "mercury level in otter" to "mercury and otter," or add alternatives ("seafood or fish").

- Give both the abbreviation and the full name, linked by *"or"* (*CIA* or *Central Intelligence Agency*).

- You may need to try a different search engine or database.

- The information may be there, but your computer cannot reach it at this time. Try later.

Too Many Listings

- Take a look at the first ten results to see if they coincide at all with your topic. For instance, if your inquiry on the Chrysler Building yielded thousands of articles, and the first ten are all about cars, you'll need to rephrase the search.

- If the first ten listings are on your topic, skim a few of them to extract more search terms.

- Add more words to your search string, using *and* or the plus sign (+) between terms. Be aware that some search engines read "+" as a command to show only documents including that specific word.

    "Chrysler Building"+architect+"New York"+"Art Deco"+Design

    Note that quotation marks are used around phrases. Also try putting a more specific word first.

- Use *not* or the minus sign (–) in front of terms that you do not want.

    "Chrysler Building"–automobile–"car dealer"–Detroit

◼ Other Library Resources

Media Section

Here you can see slides, filmstrips, and videotapes; listen to records or compact discs; look at slides under microscopes; and listen to foreign language tapes. All of these resources are indexed in the library catalog.

The Pamphlet File

Somewhere in almost every library is the pamphlet file (sometimes called the *vertical file* or *clip file*). In this file are housed years and years of clippings and accumulations of pamphlets—all sorts of information about a variety of subjects. The pamphlet file is an especially good source of material pertaining to local areas such as your state or hometown. You'll need to ask a librarian for access.

Interlibrary Loan

During your research—particularly on the Internet—you may come across sources of interest that are not available in your library. At your request and with enough time, your library can obtain copies of books and photocopies of articles from other libraries.

Writing Research Papers

Here it is again, that terrifying request from a teacher for a "research" or "term" paper. Don't be scared by the names of these papers. A research or term paper is simply a fairly long paper in which you set forth a point of view and support it with outside sources of information.

The trouble with many student papers is that they present information one source at a time, pretty much copying from the sources and changing a few words. Instead, a good research paper presents *your* view of the topic, guiding the reader one idea at a time into what you have come to understand. Even in an "objective" research paper, you are your reader's guide to the subject.

This chapter gives you a step-by-step method for producing a research paper that makes sense.

■ First Steps

Before Beginning Research, Freewrite about the Topic

To discover your preliminary main point, write nonstop for about fifteen minutes without worrying about organization. Include the reasons you're interested in this subject, what you already know about it, and questions you'd like to answer.

Narrow Your Topic

Before searching for reading materials, limit what you'll attempt to cover; otherwise, you will read yourself into a hole and never get your paper written. One method is to write a controlling sentence that will explain and limit your paper. (Teachers sometimes call this sentence a *thesis statement* or a *topic sentence*.) You may sometimes have to use two sentences, but try for one.

> Pizza is the most wholesome fast food on the American market today.

Network

Tell your family and friends that you're looking for information; ask them to save articles for you and to listen for reports on the radio or television.

■ DURING RESEARCH

Search for Supporting Information

Now is the time to choose your reading. Study carefully the chapter on "Using the College Library and the Internet" (pages 97–103). Get an overview of what is available in the library before you actually start reading. You can also ask someone who knows the field for suggestions about what's best to read. You can take an hour to browse on the World Wide Web. You can check bibliographies in the backs of books. It can be exciting to follow the leads that you discover as you search for information. Also, don't overlook other sources such as

- Local organizations
- Interviews with experts
- Radio, television, and videos
- A visit to an institution

- Your family
- Your classmates
- Local libraries
- Businesses

Take Notes from Your Reading

After you've written down a few key questions, focus your reading on answering those questions. Remember that you want to gather supporting information, not copy other people's words. Be aware that you cannot write your paper while taking notes. These must be two separate steps.

- First, write down the details about your source that you will need for your Works Cited page.

  For a book: author, title, place of publication, publisher, and date of publication

  For an article: author, title of article, title of publication, date, and pages

For an article on the Internet: author (if given), title of article (or type of article if E-mail or posting to a bulletin board), complete Internet address, and date you viewed it.

A good method is to keep an index card for each source with all this information; then when you type your Works Cited page, you can simply shuffle the cards into alphabetical order.

- Next, take notes *sparingly* as you read. Take notes in phrases, not whole sentences. You will run yourself crazy if you try to take down every word, and your notes will be harder for you to read. It's best to read a number of paragraphs, then summarize them in your own words. Immediately write the source (author's last name and page number will do it). If a quotation strikes you as well said or interesting, copy it word for word and put quotation marks around it in your notes.

A word about copying to your disk or photocopying: Copying is a real time saver, but it complicates your task of avoiding plagiarism. Use a separate file for each item copied electronically. After you've finished, go back and mark each file (perhaps with a distinctive typeface, or with a note to yourself at the beginning of each and every paragraph) so you will recognize that *every word* is copied (plagiarized). This material cannot be used honestly in your own paper *as is* but must be carefully quoted from, paraphrased, or summarized. Of course, you will be able to see that a photocopy is not your own writing, but you still must be able to tell where it came from; so immediately write the publication information on the photocopy.

In any case, a photocopy or a copy to your disk is not a substitute for notes. When you take notes, you are taking a step toward putting the information you've found into your own words.

If you get an insight of your own, as you are reading, stop and write about it. Remember, you need to develop your own opinions and thoughts about your subject.

After you've finished taking all your notes, go back over them and mark the important points with an asterisk or with a highlighting pen. You might also find it helpful to make a brief outline or a short summary from each of your sources.

■ WRITING THE PAPER

Discover Your Own Perspective

After you have read and understood your sources, put your notes, books, and magazines aside in order to find your own position. Spend time freewriting or listing ideas until you know what you think about the topic. You might go back to the sentence you wrote before you began your research—the controlling idea. Is this still your main point? If not, write a new one.

Organize Your Material and Write a First Draft

Without consulting your notes, develop a short informal outline. Put all the major points you plan to make into a logical arrangement. Avoid merely giving a part of your paper to each source you read; instead, give a part to each of the points you want to make.

Write a draft of your entire paper. Do this also without consulting your notes or your sources, just from memory. Be sure to include a paragraph for each topic in your informal outline. Explain information as you understand it; don't check the details yet.

Write to persuade. Remember that you are the authority. Use the facts that you remember to back up your position. Anticipate the reader's questions and doubts, and respond to them ahead of time.

Don't try for fancy words and long sentences. Tell what you know, emphasizing in your own words what is most important.

Incorporate Your Sources into Your Paper

Now you can consult your notes. Read them and see which notes relate to the main points of your first draft. Look for strong quotations and facts that fit your main points, but don't feel you have to fit in everything you've found.

You may discover a whole main point that you left out of your first draft. If so, find the right place to include it in your paper.

Select from your notes only the support you need for your own points. Eliminate material that does not pertain to your main points.

Use your sources to expand each of your paragraphs. If you can, use several sources of information in explaining each major point. Whenever you use an opinion or fact, make a note of the source and the exact page where you found it.

Relate each quotation or fact to the point you are making.

Vary the Way You Use Your Sources

There are three major ways of presenting information: *direct quotation, paraphrase,* and *summary.*

Direct Quotation

In direct quotation, you use the *exact* wording from your material and surround the words with quotation marks. Even if you use only a phrase or a key word, you must indicate that it has been taken from another source by placing it within quotation marks.

Direct quotation often is overused in papers. Your paper should not be more than fifteen percent quotation.

- *Do quote:*

  Memorable and distinctive phrases
  Strong statements of opinion by authorities

- *Do not quote:*

  Facts and statistics *(He was born in 1945.)*
  Standard terminology in a field *(asthma, velocity)*

  Avoid relying too heavily on quotation by consciously using the other two methods of *paraphrase* and *summary.*

  The sections on "Quotation Marks" and "How to Quote from Your Sources" will help you with the correct form for quotations and will also give you ideas for leading into quotations and making sure they fit smoothly into your paragraphs.

Paraphrase

When you paraphrase, you take someone else's idea or information and put it into your own words. Usually you paraphrase one statement, not more than a few lines, at one time. A good place for paraphrase, rather than quotation, is in telling basic facts: dates, statistics, places, etc. The pitfall in paraphrasing comes when you stick too closely to your source's phrasing, writing things you don't fully understand in language not really your own. Instead, read the passage (making sure you understand it), close the book, and write your paraphrase in plain English.

You can't half paraphrase. That is, if you mix in some of the author's exact words, you must use quotation marks around them.

Summary

When you summarize, you take a substantial amount of material and condense it. You can summarize a long passage, several pages, a chapter, or even an entire article or book. Use summary when you want to acknowledge a conflicting idea or when you want to cover a related idea without too much detail.

Incorporate Any Visuals You Plan to Use

Don't just stick in a visual for effect. First be certain that the illustration gives additional information or clarifies a statement in your paper. It has to have a purpose.

Be sure that your illustration is clear. Enlarge it if you need to.

Give each visual a title and place it into the text right at the point where you have discussed it; however, if the visuals will be too disruptive to the paper, add them in an appendix at the end.

If you did not create the visual, see page 116 for correct documentation.

■ FINAL STEPS

Revise Your Essay

Copying over a first draft is not revising. Careful revision requires several steps:

- **Make sure that you have written clearly**—not in an artificial style.

- **Check that each paragraph has one clear point** and is logically connected to the paragraphs before and after it. Omit or move information that doesn't fit with a paragraph's main point.

- **Look for places where the reader will need more information** in order to follow your point.

- **Check for smoothness** leading into and out of direct quotations, paraphrases, and summaries.

Edit Your Essay

Make corrections before you type, and proofread the final copy as well. Check the following aspects of your paper:

- Manuscript format (see pages 85–87)

- Accuracy and punctuation of quotations (see pages 41–44)

- Format of documentation (see pages 112–125)

- The basics: spelling, punctuation, etc.

Plagiarism (Cheating)

Penalties for plagiarism can be severe: failure of the course or expulsion from the college. Unintentional plagiarism is still plagiarism, so be careful and know the rules.

Plagiarism means *writing facts, quotations, or opinions that you got from someone else without identifying your source; or using someone else's words without putting quotation marks around them.*

To Avoid Plagiarism

- Always give credit for a fact, quotation, or opinion whether you read it, retrieved it electronically, saw it on television, heard it on the radio, or learned it from another person—even when you use your own wording.

- When you use another person's wording—even a phrase—always put quotation marks around the person's exact words.

- Write your first draft with your books closed. Do not write with a book or magazine open next to you. Don't go back and forth taking ideas from a source and writing your paper.

- Don't let your sources take over the essay. Tell what you know well in your own style, stressing what you find most important.

DOCUMENTATION

The word *documentation* means that you have added two elements to your paper:

> Citations of Sources
> List of Works Cited

■ CITATIONS

When you give citations in a paper, you tell specifically where you got a piece of information—in other words, the *source* you used.

WHEN TO GIVE YOUR SOURCE

You must acknowledge in your paper the source of

- A direct quotation

- A statistic

- An idea

- Someone else's opinion

- Concrete facts

- Information taken from a computer

- Illustrations, photographs, or charts—if not your own

- Information not commonly known

Even if you *paraphrase* (put someone else's words into your own words) or *summarize* (condense someone else's words or ideas), you still must acknowledge the source of your information.

If a fact is common knowledge (George Washington was the first president), you don't have to give your source.

HOW TO USE PARENTHETICAL CITATION

These days *footnotes* and *endnotes*—with little numbers above the lines—are used less and less. The current method—known as the MLA (Modern Language Association) Style—uses *parenthetical citation.* In this system you give your source in parentheses immediately after you give the information. Your reader can then find the complete listing of each source at the end of the paper in your Works Cited section.

The four most common citations are

- Author and page number
- Title and page number
- Page number only
- Secondhand quotations

Author and Page Number

Put the author's last name and the page number in parentheses immediately after the information:

> (Schrambling 125).

Notice that there is no "p." and no comma. In the text it looks like this:

> Tex-Mex flavored pizza has become very popular (Schrambling 125).

If your citation comes at the end of a sentence, the period goes outside the last parenthesis. (Exception: With indented quotations, the period goes before the parentheses.)

Where a page number is not available, give the number of a section (sec.), paragraph (para.), or line (l.) if possible.

Title and Page Number

Often articles, editorials, pamphlets, and other materials have no author listed. In such cases, give only the first distinctive word of the title followed by the page number:

> The actual fat content of a frozen pizza may be more than the package claims ("A Meal" 19).

Note that you give the title of the specific article that you read, not the title of the newspaper, magazine, or reference book ("A Meal" not <u>Consumer Reports</u>).

Page Number Only

Put only the page number in parentheses when you have already mentioned the author's name.

> Jim Cohen makes low-fat pizzas "from start to finish on the grill" (93).

When possible, use this method of citation. Mentioning the author's name as you present information makes your paper more cohesive and readable.

Secondhand Quotations

When you quote someone who has been quoted in one of your sources, use *qtd. in* (quoted in):

> Evelyne Slomon, author of numerous cookbooks, refers to the years between 1920 and the early 50s as the "golden age of pizza in America" (qtd. in O'Neill 59).

In this example Slomon said it, although you found it in O'Neill. Note that Slomon will not be listed in your Works Cited; O'Neill will be.

Special Cases

Electronic Sources

- Articles and books originally in print

  For sources originally in print but read on the screen or printed from the computer, follow the same format as you would for the printed versions, but without page numbers. In your Works Cited you will indicate where you found the source—either CD-ROM or the Internet address.

  > Another way to reduce fat in deep-dish pizza is by substituting turkey sausage and part-skim mozzarella (Gooch).

- Other electronic sources—including Web sites, online postings, videos, and television or radio programs.

Most electronic sources do not have page numbers. You may give the name in parentheses, but you can be more precise by indicating the format and incorporating the speaker or organization smoothly into your sentence.

> In a discussion of how to reduce the fat content of traditional pizza recipes, Jim Powers posted a suggestion: substitute a fat-free flour tortilla for the pizza crust.

> Professor Carlo Mangone, who teaches nutrition at the Second University of Naples, said in a recent radio interview that there are only two classic pizzas–the marinara and the margherita.

Interview or Speech

If your source is an interview, lecture, or speech, include the person's name in your paragraph and use no parenthetical citation.

> Kevin O'Reilly, owner of K. O'Reilly's Pizza, reports that pepperoni pizza outsells the low-fat versions ten to one.

Two Sources by the Same Author

When you have two or more sources by the same author, use the first identifying words to indicate the title of the work you're citing.

> Julia Child advises that the dough be chilled to slow the rising (In Julia's 6).

> or

> Some chefs chill the dough to slow the rising (Child, In Julia's 6).

Organization as Author

Sometimes the author is an organization.

> According to the United States Department of Agriculture, one slice of cheese pizza has 165 calories (1).

> or

> One slice of cheese pizza has 165 calories (United States Dept. of Agriculture 1).

Note: Do not abbreviate in your sentence—only in the parenthetical citation.

Illustration or Graphics

- If the artist's name is given and the visual (such as an editorial cartoon) is not an illustration of the text surrounding it, put the last name and page number in parentheses below the graphic.

  (Chaney 69).

- If the artist's name is given but the visual illustrates the text with which it appears, give the artist's name and then the author's name and the page.

  (Acevedo in Cohen 97).

  Note that only Cohen will be listed in your Works Cited.

- If the artist is not identified (for instance, in an advertisement) give the author (or owner of the copyright) and page where the illustration appeared.

  (Kraft Foods 5).

HOW OFTEN TO GIVE CITATIONS

When several facts in a row within one paragraph all come from the same page of a source, use one citation to cover them all. Place the citation after the last fact, but alert the reader at the outset with a phrase such as "According to Janet Tynan, . . ."

Do not, however, wait more than a few lines to let the reader know where the facts came from. The citation must be in the same paragraph as the facts.

Remember: You must give citations for information, not just for quotations.

SAMPLE PARAGRAPH USING CITATIONS

On the following page is a sample paragraph in which you can see how various citations are used. (You will rarely have this many citations in one short paragraph.) The sources cited here can be found among the works cited on page 125.

When the first pizzeria opened in New York City in 1905 ("Pizza" 490), it introduced the classic Italian pizza—bread dough covered with tomato sauce and cheese. Now, almost a century later, the simple pizza has been transformed into an American creation that reflects this country's love of diversity. In addition to the classic version, pizza lovers can now savor just about every combination and concoction imaginable. The National Association of Pizza Operators reports that "Pizza makers have tried virtually every type of food on pizzas, including peanut butter and jelly, bacon and eggs, and mashed potatoes" (qtd. in "A Meal" 21). Gourmet versions, such as the Tex-Mex, which Regina Schrambling says is "welcomed by most Americans" (125), continue to satisfy our taste for the unusual. From France comes the pissaladière, which adds fresh herbs, black olives, and anchovies to the lowly pizza (Child, Bertholle, and Beck 151). A chef from Utah, Julie Wilson, offers a high-brow combination made with blue cheese and fresh pears (Claiborne and Franey 70). You might have to travel to Italy to get real Italian pizza, but you can eat your way across this country sampling several hundred modern versions of pizza made the American way.

■ WORKS CITED

When you were gathering your material, you may have used a "working *bibliography*," a list of potential sources. However, now that you have written your paper and have seen which sources you actually did use, you must include at the end of the paper a list of Works Cited.

There are four major points to understand about a Works Cited page:

- List *only* those sources that you actually referred to in your paper.

- List the whole article, or essay, or book—not just the pages you used.

- *Alphabetize* your list of sources by the authors' last names. If no author is listed, alphabetize by the first main word in the title.

- Format is extremely important to many teachers. Pay special attention to order, spacing, and punctuation.

  - ~ Put the author's last name first.

  - ~ Double-space the entire list.

  - ~ Start each entry at the left margin.

  - ~ Indent the second and third lines of each entry five spaces.

  - ~ Notice that most of the items in a citation are separated by periods.

  - ~ Leave one space after a comma or colon, two spaces after a period (except after an abbreviation).

  - ~ Put a period at the end of each entry.

SPECIFIC ENTRIES

Book

Author. <u>Title</u>. City: Publisher, date.

```
Love, Louise. The Complete Book of Pizza.
        Evanston, IL: Sassafras, 1980.
```

Note: If the city of publication is not well known, give the abbreviation for the state.

Article in a Magazine

Author. "Title of Article." Title of Periodical Date: page(s).

> Schrambling, Regina. "Tex-Mex Pizza." Working
> Woman Feb. 1988: 125.

Article in a Newspaper

Author (if given). "Title of Article." Title of Newspaper Complete
date, section: page(s).

> Claiborne, Craig, and Pierre Franey. "Feasts
> against Frost." New York Times 17 Jan.
> 1988, sec. 6: 69-70.

Article or Story in a Collection or Anthology

Author of article. "Title of Article." Title of Book. Editor of book.
City: Publisher, date. Pages covered by article.

> Cook, Joan Marble. "Italy: Myths and Truths."
> Italy. Ed. Ronald Steel. New York:
> Wilson, 1963. 31-37.

Article in a Scholarly Journal

Author. "Title of Article." Title of Journal Volume number (Complete
date): pages covered by article.

> Larson, D. M., et al. "The Effects of Flour
> Type and Dough Retardation Time on
> Sensory Characteristics of Pizza Crust."
> Cereal Chemistry 70 (Nov.-Dec. 1993):
> 647-50.

Material from Computers

Note: If complete information about your source is not available—for example, the name of the author—just list whatever information you have, in the order given below, without blank spaces.

Standalone Database or CD-ROM

Author. "Title." [or the heading of the material you read] <u>Title of the entire work</u> and publishing information of original in print, if known. <u>Title of the database</u>. Publication medium. Vendor (if relevant). Electronic publication date.

```
Gooch, Annette. "Deep-Dish Dough: Leaner
     Chicago-Style Pizza from Scratch."
     Newsday 16 Mar. 1997 sec. Food Day: 1.
     Newsbank Newsday. CD-ROM. 1997.
```

Online Source or Website

Author or organization. "Title of the article." <u>Title of the complete work</u>. Date of publication or last revision. Sponsoring organization if different from author. Date you viewed it <address of the Website>.

```
United States. Dept. of Agriculture.
     "Nutritional Data for 100 grams of
     Entrees; Pizza with Cheese." USDA
     Nutrient Values. 31 Aug. 1997.
     13 Oct. 1997 <http://www.rahul.net/
     cgi-bin/fatfree/usda/usda-10cgi?
     ENTREESx%20PIZZA%20WITH%20CHEESE>.
```

Direct E-Mail to You (not a discussion group)

Author of E-mail [title or area of expertise, professional affiliation]. "Subject line." E-mail to the author [meaning you] date.

```
Brooks, Evelyn [Marketing researcher,
     Moorpark, CA, Food Association].
     "Re: Pizza." E-mail to the author. 12
     Oct. 1997.
```

Posting to a Discussion Group

Real name of author. "The subject line of the article." Online posting. The date of the posting. The group to which it was sent—if there are multiple groups, separate them by a comma. Date you viewed it <where the article can be retrieved>.

```
Powers, Jim. "Re: Low-Fat Pizza." Online
     posting. 10 May 1997. alt.food.low-fat.
     2 June 1997 <http://xp6.dejanews.com/
     getdoc.xp?recnum=6332052&server=
     dbbb97p2x&CONTEXT=8>.
```

Encyclopedia

"Title of Article." Title of Encyclopedia. Year of the edition.

```
"Pizza." Encyclopaedia Britannica:
     Micropaedia. 1997 ed.
```

Special Cases

No Author Listed

Alphabetize according to the first main word of the title. Include *A, An, The,* but do not use them when alphabetizing. For example, this article will be alphabetized with *M* in the Works Cited:

```
"A Meal That's Easy as Pie: How to Pick a
     Pizza That's Good and Healthful."
     Consumer Reports Jan. 1997: 19-23.
```

Two or More Authors

Give the last name first for the first author only; use first name first for the other author(s).

```
Child, Julia, Louisette Bertholle, and Simone
     Beck. Mastering the Art of French
     Cooking. Vol. 1. New York: Knopf, 1966.
```

Additional Works by the Same Author

Use three hyphens and a period in place of the author's name and alphabetize the works by title.

> Child, Julia. <u>In Julia's Kitchen with Master</u>
> <u>Chefs</u>. New York: Knopf, 1995.
> ---. <u>Julia Child and More Company</u>. New York:
> Ballantine, 1979.

Pamphlet

Follow the format for a book. Often an organization is the publisher. If no author is listed, begin with the title. If no date is listed, use n.d. for no date.

> United States. Dept. of Agriculture. <u>Eating</u>
> <u>Better When Eating Out: Using the Dietary</u>
> <u>Guidelines</u>. Washington: GPO, n.d.

Radio or Television Program

Give the name of the speaker. Underline the title of the program. Give the network, if any, then the station call letters and city. Then list the date of the broadcast.

> Mangone, Carlo. <u>Weekend Edition Saturday</u>.
> Natl. Public Radio. WNYC, New York.
> 31 May 1997.

Videocassette or Audio Recording

List the author, director, or performer; the title; the format; the distributor; and the release date.

> Claiborne, Craig. <u>Craig Claiborne's New York</u>
> <u>Times Video Cookbook</u>. Videocassette.
> New York Times Productions, 1985.

Interview, Speech, or Lecture

Give the person's name and position, the kind of presentation (personal or telephone interview, speech, or classroom lecture), the location, and the date.

```
O'Reilly, Kevin [Owner, K O'Reilly's Pizza].
    Personal interview. Troy, MO.
    19 Oct. 1997.
```

Illustration or Graphics

- If the artist's name is given and the visual (such as an editorial cartoon) is not an illustration of the text surrounding it, give the artist's name, the type of visual it is (cartoon, photograph, chart), and the complete information for the source in which it appears, including the date viewed or the page.

```
Chaney, Tom. Cartoon. New Yorker 30 Jan.
    1989: 69.
```

- If the artist's name is given but the visual illustrates the text with which it appears, give only the author and other information for the text.

```
Cohen, Jim. "Simple, Healthful Grilling."
    Food & Wine June 1997: 92-98+.
```

- If the artist is not identified (for instance, in an advertisement) give the author (or owner of the copyright) and complete information on the source, including the page where the illustration appeared.

```
Kraft Foods. Advertisement. Eating Well
    July/Aug. 1997: 5.
Cedarlane Natural Foods. Chart. Low Fat
    Vegetarian Pizza Veggie Wrap. 31 July
    1997. 7 Aug. 1997 <http://www.cedarlane
    foods.com/p00ag.htm>.
```

A sample of a Works Cited page follows. It illustrates a variety of sources and therefore is longer than you probably will need. The left-hand page identifies the category of each source.

Explanations of Works Cited

Book, single author ————————————————————————

Repeated author (same author as above) ————————————

Book, three authors, one volume cited, (repeated author with first
citing of co-authors) ——————————————————————

Newspaper article ——————————————————————————

Article or chapter in an edited collection [Use this form also for a
single selection from an anthology.] ——————————————

Article in a scholarly journal, more than three authors ————————

Radio program [Use this form also for a television program.] ————

Magazine article (monthly), unsigned ——————————————

Interview [Use this form also for a lecture or speech.] ——————————

Encyclopedia article, unsigned ————————————————————

Magazine article, signed ——————————————————————

Article on the Internet, organization as author ——————————

Works Cited

Child, Julia. <u>In Julia's Kitchen with Master Chefs</u>. New York: Knopf, 1995.

---. <u>Julia Child and More Company</u>. New York: Ballantine, 1979.

Child, Julia, Louisette Bertholle, and Simone Beck. <u>Mastering the Art of French Cooking</u>. Vol. 1. New York: Knopf, 1966.

Claiborne, Craig, and Pierre Franey. "Feasts against Frost." <u>New York Times</u> 17 Jan. 1988, sec. 6: 69–70.

Cook, Joan Marble. "Italy: Myths and Truths." <u>Italy</u>. Ed. Ronald Steel. New York: Wilson, 1963, 31–37.

Larsen, D. M., et al. "The Effects of Flour Type and Dough Retardation Time on Sensory Characteristics of Pizza Crust." <u>Cereal Chemistry</u> 70 (1993): 647–50.

Mangone, Carlo. <u>Weekend Edition Saturday</u>. Natl. Public Radio. WNYC, New York. 31 May 1997.

"A Meal That's Easy as Pie: How to Pick a Pizza That's Good and Healthful." <u>Consumer Reports</u> Jan. 1997: 19–23.

O'Reilly, Kevin [Owner, K O'Reilly's Pizza]. Personal Interview. Troy, MO. 19 Oct. 1997.

"Pizza." <u>Encyclopaedia Britannica: Micropaedia</u>. 1997 ed.

Schrambling, Regina. "Tex-Mex Pizza." <u>Working Woman</u> Feb. 1988: 125.

United States. Dept. of Agriculture. "Nutritional Data for 100 grams of Entrees; Pizza with Cheese." <u>USDA Nutrient Values</u>. 31 Aug. 1997. 13 Oct. 1997. <http://www.rahul.net/cgi-bin/ fatfree/usda/usda-10cgi?ENTREESx%20PIZZA %20WITH%20CHEESE>.

PART 4

WRITING WITH ELEGANCE

Keeping a Journal
Finding Your Voice
Adding Details
Recognizing Clichés
Eliminating Biased Language
Trimming Wordiness
Varying Your Sentences
Postscript

Keeping a Journal

Keeping a journal is one of the best ways to grow as a writer. A journal helps you put your thoughts and feelings into words, helps you overcome writer's block, and helps you develop your own personal style. You will also discover truths you didn't know—about yourself and about many topics. Some of your journal writing can later be developed into complete essays or stories.

Make your journal a record of your inward journey. Don't make it a diary—a day-by-day list of what you do. Instead, set down your memories, your feelings, your observations, your hopes. A journal gives you the opportunity to try your hand at different types of writing, so aim for variety in your entries.

Some Guidelines for Keeping a Journal

- Write several times a week for at least ten minutes.

- Use a notebook you really like. Write in ink. Date each entry.

- If you have no topic, write whatever comes into your head or choose one of the suggestions from the list given here.

- While you write, don't worry about correctness. Write as spontaneously and as honestly as you can, and let your thoughts and words flow freely.

- At your leisure, re-read your entries and make any corrections or additions you like. Remember, this journal is for *you*, and it will be a source of delight to you in years to come.

Some Suggestions for Journal Entries

Blow off steam.

Describe someone you love.

Tell your favorite story about yourself when you were little.

State a controversial opinion and then defend your position.

Respond to a movie, a TV program, a book, an article, a concert, a song.

Write a letter to someone and say what you can't say face to face.

Describe in full detail a place you know and love.

Remember on paper your very first boyfriend or girlfriend.

Make a list of all the things you want to do.

Immortalize one of your enemies in writing.

Relate, using present tense, a memorable dream you've had.

Sit in front of a drawing or painting and write down the feelings and images it evokes in you.

Analyze the personal trait that gets you in trouble most often.

Relate an incident in which you were proud (or ashamed) of yourself.

Describe your dream house.

Capture on paper some object—such as a toy or article of clothing—that you loved as a child.

Go all the way back: Try to remember your very first experience in the world and describe how it looked to you then.

Make a list of your accomplishments.

Write down a family story. Include when and where you have heard it.

Choose something you'd like to know more about—or need to know more about—and tell why.

Tell about your favorite meal, food, or recipe.

Set down a "here and now" scene: Record sensory details right at the moment you're experiencing them.

Go to a public place and observe people. Write down your observations.

Explain your most pressing problem at present.

Describe your very favorite article of clothing and tell why it means so much to you.

Analyze your relationship to food.

Write about a relative whom you now think of differently from the way you did when you were a child.

Take an abstract idea such as delight, grief, or pride, and write down very specifically what the idea means to you.

Explain exactly how to do some activity you know well. Use sketches if you need to illustrate or clarify your point.

Write about yourself as a writer.

Trace the history of your hair.

Take one item from today's newspaper and give your thoughts about it.

Commit yourself in writing to doing something you've always wanted to do but never have.

Explain how you feel about fighting.

Tell about something that happened at least two years ago that you still wonder about. Include the questions in your mind and some possible answers.

Finding Your Voice

Often we write the way we think we're supposed to, with big words and fancy sentences. The writing comes out awkward and impersonal. But good writing has the feel of a real person talking.

To find your own voice as a writer, keep these questions in mind when you write:

Am I saying this in plain English?

Are these words that I normally use?

Am I saying what I know to be true instead of what I think others want to hear?

A great technique for developing your own voice is to read your work aloud. If you do it regularly, you'll begin to notice when other voices are intruding or when you are using roundabout phrases. In time, your sentences will gain rhythm and force. Reading aloud helps you to remember that, when you write, you are telling something to somebody. In fact, another good technique is to visualize a particular person and pretend you are writing directly to that person.

Good writing is *honest.* Honest writing requires you to break through your fears of what other people might think of you and to tell what you know to be true. Your readers will appreciate the truth, shared with simplicity by a writer who has given the topic attention and has decided what is important.

Adding Details

Details give life to your ideas. As you write, you naturally concentrate on your ideas, but the reader will best remember a strong example or fact.

Adding Information

If a teacher asks for "more details," you probably have written a generalization with insufficient support. You need to slow down, take *one* idea at a time, and tell what it is based upon. You cannot assume that the reader agrees with you or knows what you're talking about. You have to say where you got your idea. This comes down to adding some of the following details to support your point:

- Examples

- Facts

- Logical reasoning

- Explanation of abstract words

Ideas are abstract and hard to picture. To be remembered, they must be embodied in concrete language—in pictures, in facts, in things that happened.

For example, here are three abstract statements:

> Gloria means what she says.
> The scene in the film was romantic.
> The paramecium displayed peculiar behavior.

Now here they are made more concrete:

> Gloria means what she says. She says she hates television, and she backs it up by refusing to date any man who watches TV.

> The soft focus of the camera and the violin music in the background heightened the romance of the scene.

> Under the microscope, the paramecium displayed peculiar behavior. It doubled in size and turned purple.

Adding Sensory Details

The best writing appeals to our five senses. Your job as a writer is to put down words that will cause the reader to see, hear, smell, taste, or feel exactly what you experienced.

You can sharpen your senses with "here and now" exercises.

- Observe and write exactly what you see, feel, smell, taste, and hear moment by moment. Expand your descriptions until they become very specific.

- Write a paragraph describing a memory you have of a smell, a taste, a sight, a sound, a feeling (either a touch or a sensation).

- Take one object—an orange, a frying pan, a leaf—and describe it completely, using as many sensory details as possible.

These exercises will help build the habit of including careful observation in your writing.

Recognizing Clichés

A cliché is a *predictable* word, phrase, or statement. If it sounds very familiar, if it comes very easily, it's probably a cliché. Clichés are comfortable—often so old that they are in our bones—and they are usually true.

In conversation, clichés are often acceptable, but in writing they either annoy or bore the reader. Learn to recognize clichés and replace them with fresher, sharper language.

Recognize Clichés

The best way to spot clichés is to make a list of all the ones you hear. Clichés fall into groups:

- Comparisons

Cold as ice	Slept like a log
Drunk as a skunk	Fought like a tiger
Hot as . . .	Smooth as silk

- Pairs

Hot and heavy	By leaps and bounds
Apples and oranges	Wining and dining

- Images

    Makes my blood boil
    A chip off the old block
    A beached whale
    Your room is a pigsty.
    Between a rock and a hard place

- Sayings

    There are other fish in the sea.
    Read my lips.
    No use crying over spilt milk.
    Join the club.
    Been there, done that.

- Lines

    What's a nice girl like you doing in a place like this?
    Haven't I met you somewhere before?
    We've got to stop meeting like this.

- Phrases

    Madly in love
    Ripe old age
    Easier said than done

- "In" words

    User-friendly
    Cool

This year's new expression is next year's cliché. (Try saying "groovy" to your friends.)

People use clichés when they have to play it safe—making conversation or writing for an unfamiliar teacher. Uncomfortable situations invite clichés—first dates, beginnings of parties, funerals.

Eliminate Clichés

- Often you can simply omit a cliché—you don't need it. The essay is better without it.

- At other times, replace the cliché by saying what you mean. Give the details.

- Look out for clichés in your conclusion; that's where they love to gather.

- Make up your own comparisons and descriptions. Have fun writing creatively from your own viewpoint and sensations. You might start by rewriting some of the clichés in this chapter.

ELIMINATING BIASED LANGUAGE

Biased language includes all expressions that demean or exclude people. To avoid offending your reader, examine both the words you use and their underlying assumptions.

Offensive Word Choices

Some wording is prejudiced or impolite or outdated:

Eliminate name-calling, slurs, or derogatory nicknames. Instead, refer to groups by the names they use for themselves. For example, use *women* (not *chicks*), *African Americans* (not *colored people*), *Native Americans* (not *Indians*).

Replace words using *man* or the *-ess* ending with nonsexist terms. For example, use *flight attendant* (not *stewardess*), *mechanic* (not *repairman*), *leader* or *diplomat* (not *statesman*), *humanity* (not *mankind*).

False Assumptions

Some statements are based on hidden biases. Look hard at references to any group—even one you belong to. Acknowledge that every member of the group does not believe or look or behave exactly like every other member.

Check for stereotyping about innate abilities or flaws in members of a group. For example, all women are not maternal, all lawyers are not devious, all Southerners are not racist, and all Japanese are not industrious. Many clichés are based in stereotypes: *absent-minded professor, dumb jock, Latin temper.*

Check assumptions that certain jobs are best filled by certain ethnic groups or one sex: For example, all nurses aren't women; all mechanics aren't men; all ballet dancers aren't Russian.

Watch for inconsistency.

- In a pair:

   man and wife

Instead, use

   man and woman   or   husband and wife

- In a list:

   two Republicans, a Democrat, an Independent, a woman, and
   an African American

This list assumes that everyone is a white man unless otherwise
specified.

Instead, use

   three Republicans, two Democrats, and an Independent

Faulty Pronoun Usage

Check pronouns for bias.

   Each Supreme Court justice should have *his clerk* attend the
   conference.

- One option for revision is to use *his* or *her*

   Each Supreme Court justice should have *his* or *her* clerk attend
   the conference.

- A better solution is to use the plural throughout

   Supreme Court justices should have *their* clerks attend the
   conference.

- Often the most graceful solution is to eliminate the pronoun

   Each Supreme Court justice should have a clerk attend the
   conference.

You can find more help with pronoun choice in the section
"Consistent Pronouns" (see pages 19–21).

Trimming Wordiness

Often we think that people are impressed by a writer who uses big words and long sentences. Actually, people are more impressed by a writer who is *clear*.

Cut Empty Words

Some words sound good but carry no clear meaning. Omitting them will often make the sentence sharper.

experience	proceeded to
situation	the fact that
is a man who	really
personality	thing
in today's society	something

In the following examples, the first version is wordy; the second version is trim.

The fire was a terrifying situation and a depressing experience for all of us.
The fire terrified and depressed all of us.

Carmen is a person who has a tempestuous personality.
Carmen is tempestuous.

The reason she quit was because of the fact that she was sick.
She quit because of illness.

Anger is something we all feel.
We all feel anger.

Avoid Redundancy—Pointless Repetition

He married his wife twelve years ago.
He married twelve years ago.

She wore a scarf that was pink in color.
She wore a pink scarf.

Be Direct

Tell what something *is*, rather than what it *isn't*.

> Captain Bligh was not a very nice man.
> Captain Bligh was vicious.

Replace Fancy or Technical Words

You can replace *abode* with *house* and *coronary thrombosis* with *heart attack* and bring your paper down to earth. Some subjects may require technical language, but in general, strive to use everyday words.

Get Rid of *Being* Verbs

Being verbs like *is* and *are* sap the energy from your writing. They dilute your sentences. Often you can replace *being* verbs with forceful verbs.

Look out for *am, is, are, was, were, be, being, been*.

Especially watch out for *there is, there are, there were, it is, it was*.

Go through your paper and circle all of these limp verbs. Replace them with dynamic verbs. This exercise produces a dramatic difference in any writing. Don't give up easily. Sometimes you will have to rewrite or combine several sentences. Sometimes you will have to make a sentence much more precise.

> There are three people who influenced my career.
> Three people influenced my career.
>
> Michael was living in the past.
> Michael lived in the past.
>
> It is depressing to watch the local news.
> Watching the local news depresses me.
>
> His walk was unsteady.
> He wobbled when he walked.

> The audience was irate. People were jumping out of their seats and were flooding the aisles.

> The irate audience jumped out of their seats and flooded the aisles.

Save *being* verbs for times when you actually mean state of being:

> She was born on Bastille Day.
> I think; therefore, I am.
> They were exhausted.

When you trim, don't worry that your papers will be too short: For length, add examples and further thoughts. Look at the topic from a different viewpoint. Add points, not just words.

Varying Your Sentences

The same idea can be put in many different ways, and every sentence has movable parts. To get more music or drama into your style, try reading your writing aloud. When you come across choppy or monotonous sentences, use some of the following techniques.

Write an Important Sentence Several Ways

You can turn a sentence that troubles you into a sentence that pleases you. Instead of fiddling with a word here and a word there, try writing five completely different sentences—each with the same idea. One could be long, one short, one a generalization, one a picture, and so forth. Often you'll find that your first isn't your best. If you play with several possibilities, you'll come up with the one you want. This technique works especially well for improving introductions and conclusions.

Use Short Sentences Frequently

Short sentences are the meat and bones of good writing.

- They can simplify an idea.
- They can dramatize a point.
- They can create suspense.
- They can add rhythm.
- They can be blunt and forceful.

If you're getting tangled in too many words, a few short sentences will often get you through.

Remember, however, that you must use a period even between very short but complete sentences:

> It was a rainy Monday. I was sitting at my desk. I heard a knock at the door. I waited. The doorknob turned.

Lengthen Choppy Sentences

Using *only* short sentences can make your writing monotonous. If you want to lengthen a sentence, the simplest way is to add concrete information.

> The book was boring.

> The author's long descriptions of rooms in which nothing and no one ever moved made the book boring.

Combine Choppy Sentences

Combine two short sentences back to back. Here are three ways:

- Put a semicolon between them.

> Kitty expected Anna Karenina to wear a lavender dress to the ball; Anna chose black.

(Be sure each half is a complete sentence.)

- Put a comma followed by one of these connectors:

but	and	for
or	so	yet
nor		

> Kitty expected Anna Karenina to wear a lavender dress to the ball, but Anna chose black.

- Put a semicolon followed by a transition word and a comma. Here are the most common transition words.

however	for example	meanwhile
therefore	furthermore	nevertheless
instead	in other words	on the other hand
besides		

> Kitty expected Anna Karenina to wear a lavender dress to the ball; instead, Anna chose black.

Combine sentences to highlight the major point. Often sentences contain two or more facts. You can show the relationship between these facts so that the most important one stands out.

In these examples, two ideas are given equal weight.

> Martha Grimes was a college professor. She became a best-selling mystery writer.
>
> I love Earl. He barks at the slightest sound.
>
> Brad lost a contact lens. He had one blue eye and one brown eye.

Here are the same ideas with one point emphasized.

> Before she became a best-selling mystery writer, Martha Grimes was a college professor.
>
> I love Earl even though he barks at the slightest sound.
>
> Because Brad lost a contact lens, he had one blue eye and one brown eye.

Notice that the halves of these sentences can be reversed.

> Although Earl barks at the slightest sound, I still love him.

Usually the sentence gains strength when the most interesting point comes last.

Insert the gist of one sentence inside another:

> Sheila Baldwin makes a fine living as a model. She is thin. She has high cheekbones.
>
> Sheila Baldwin, who is thin and has high cheekbones, makes a fine living as a model.

The problem with most choppy sentences is that one after another starts with the subject of the sentence—in this case, *Sheila* or *she.* Sometimes you can use *who* (for people) or *which* (for things) to start an insertion. Sometimes you can reduce the insertion to a word or two.

> I interviewed Nell Partin, who is the mayor.
> I interviewed Nell Partin, the mayor.

Give Your Sentences a Strong Ending

The beginning is worth sixty cents, what's in the middle is worth forty cents, but the end is worth a dollar.

> I walked into the room, looked around at all the flowers my friends had sent, took a deep breath, and collapsed onto the sofa in tears.

> When the nights grow cool and foggy and the full moon rises after the day's harvest, Madeline, so the story goes, roams the hills in search of revenge.

> What Louie Gallagher received, after all the plea-bargaining and haggling and postponements and hearings, was a ten-year sentence.

To stress the most important parts of your sentence, tuck in interrupters or insertions. Put transitions or minor information into the middle of your sentence.

> He argues, as you probably know, even with statues.
> From my point of view, however, that's a mistake.
> The interior decoration, designed by his cousin, looked gaudy.

Remember to put commas on *both* sides of the insertion.

Use Parallel Structure

Parallel structure—repeating certain words for clarity and emphasis—makes elegant sentences.

> To be honest is not necessarily to be brutal.

Famous quotations are often based on parallel structure.

> I came, I saw, I conquered.
>
> —Julius Caesar

> To believe your own thought, to believe that what is true for you in your private heart is true for all men—that is genius.
>
> —Ralph Waldo Emerson

> Ask not what your country can do for you; ask what you can do for your country.
>
> —John F. Kennedy

For the correct usage of parallel structure, see page 56.

Imitate Good Writers

Take a close look at the writings of some of your favorite authors. A good exercise is to pick out a sentence or a paragraph that you particularly like. Read it aloud once or twice; then copy it over several times to get the feel of the language. Now study it closely and try to write an imitation of it. Use the sentence or paragraph as a model, but think up your own ideas and words. This exercise can rapidly expand your power to vary your sentences.

Postscript

You do your best work when you take pleasure in a job. You write best when you know something about the topic and know what you want to stress. So, when you can, write about a topic you've lived with and have considered over time. When you *have* to write about a topic that seems boring or difficult, get to know it for a while, until it makes sense to you. Start with what is clear to you and you will write well.

Don't quit too soon. Sometimes a few more changes, a little extra attention to fine points, a new paragraph written on a separate piece of paper will transform an acceptable essay into an essay that really pleases you. Through the time you spend writing and rewriting, you will discover what is most important to say.

■ An Invitation

Rules of Thumb was written for you, so we welcome your comments about it and about *Good Measures: A Practice Book to Accompany Rules of Thumb*. Please write directly to us:

Jay Silverman
Elaine Hughes
Diana Roberts Wienbroer

Department of English
Nassau Community College
Garden City, New York 11530-6793

If you would like to purchase individual copies of *Rules of Thumb* directly from McGraw-Hill, please call this toll-free number:

1-800-822-8158

For textbook orders and examination copies, call:

1-800-338-3987

Visit McGraw-Hill's Higher Education Website at <www.mhhe.com>

About the Authors

A graduate of Amherst College and the University of Virginia, **Jay Silverman** has received fellowships from the Fulbright-Hayes Foundation, the Andrew Mellon Foundation, and the National Endowment for the Humanities. Dr. Silverman has taught at Virginia Highlands Community College and at Nassau Community College where he received the Honors Program Award for Excellence in Teaching and where he also teaches in the College Bound Program of the Nassau County Mental Health Association.

Elaine Hughes moved to New York City from Mississippi in 1979 to attend a National Endowment for the Humanities seminar at Columbia University. She has taught writing for more than twenty-five years, primarily at Hinds Community College in Raymond, Mississippi, and at Nassau Community College. Since her retirement from NCC and her return to Mississippi, she has conducted many writing workshops for the Esalen Institute and for other organizations. She is also the author of *Writing from the Inner Self.*

As Chair of the English Department of Nassau Community College for six years, **Diana Roberts Wienbroer** coordinated a department of 150 faculty members and served on the Executive Council of the Association of Departments of English. Besides teaching writing for over thirty years, both in Texas and New York, she has studied and taught film criticism. She is also the author of *The McGraw-Hill Guide to Electronic Research and Documentation,* 1997.

The authors have also written *Rules of Thumb for Research* and *Good Measures: A Practice Book to Accompany Rules of Thumb,* both available from McGraw-Hill.

Index

Abbreviations, 16
Abstract and concrete writing, 133–134
Agreement (singular and plural):
  of pronoun, 19–21
  subject and verb, 54
Apostrophes, 18
Authors
  documentation of, 115, 121–122
  names of, 92–93
Awkward writing:
  sentence structure, 24–25, 56–58, 142–146
  wordiness, 139–141

Biased language, 137–138
Bibliography (works cited), 118–125
Brackets, 43

Can, Could, 53
Capitalization, 14–15
CD-ROM indexes, 98–99, 120
Citations, 112–117
Clichés, 135–136
Colons
  with quotations, 41
  in works cited, 118
Commas, 35–36
  in combining sentences, 143
  comma splice (run-on sentence) 33–34
  in sentence variety, 143–144

Computer searches, 97–103, 106
Computers (Word Processors), 81, 85, 87
Conclusions, 74, 88–89
Concrete and abstract writing, 133–134
Could, Can, 53
Cover sheet, 86–87

Dangling modifiers, 57
Dashes, 39
Databases, 100, 120
Dates:
  commas in, 36
  numbers for, 17
Details, adding, 70, 76, 133–134
Development of paragraphs, 76
Diction:
  finding your voice, 132
  of pronouns:
    consistent, 19–21
    correct, 22–23
    vague, 24–25
  in sentences, tangled, 56–58
  verbs in, consistent, 51–52
Dictionary, use of, 64, 86
Dividing words at line endings, 86
Documentation, 112–125
  of a single source, 94
Drafts of paper:
  first, 61–62, 107
  second, 68–69, 107–110

–ed word endings, 54
Editing, 2, 80–81, 110
Electronic sources, 98–103,
          114–115, 120–121
Ellipsis, 43
Endnotes, 112
English as a Second Language
          (ESL), *see especially:*
   pronouns,
        correct case of, 22–23
        singular vs. plural, 19–21
        vague, 24–25
     verb agreement, 53
     verb tenses, 46–52
     word endings, 11–13, 18,
          46–53, 54–55
Essay tests, 88–90
Essays:
     format, 85–87
     organization for, 65–69
     writing about literature, 91–94
     writing from research, 104–110

Faulty sentences, 56–58
Footnotes, 112
Format of college papers, 85–87
Fragments, sentence, 26–33, 39,
          142–144
Freewriting, 61, 104

Generalizations, 133–134
Graphics, 116, 123

Had, 51
However:
     punctuation with, 33, 37
     use of, 78–79
Hyphens, 10, 86

I (pronoun),
     vs. *me,* 22–23
     use of, 20
Interlibrary loan, 103
Internet, 100–103, 114–115,
          120–121
Introductions, 72–74, 88
Italicizing, 45
Its, it's, 4, 18

Journal keeping, 129–131

Lengthening a paper, 70, 76
Library, using, 97–100, 103
Literature:
     essays about, 91–94
     quotations from, 41–44,
          95–96
     titles of, 38, 45, 92

Misplaced modifiers, 57
Mixed sentence patterns, 58

Note-taking in research,
          105–106
Numbers, 16–17

One (pronoun), 21
Online sources, 101–103,
          114–115, 120–121
Organization, 65–68
     of essay test, 88–89
     of literature essay, 91–92
     of paragraphs, 75–77
     of research paper, 107

Outlining, 65–66
  for literature essay, 91–92
  for research paper, 107

Paragraphs, 75–77
  for introductions and
      conclusions, 72–74
Parallel structure, 56, 145
Paraphrase, 108–109, 112
Parentheses, 39–40
Parenthetical citations, 94,
    112–116
Past tenses, 47, 51
Periodical section of
    library, 100
Plagiarism, 106, 111
Planning (prewriting), 65–67,
    88–89, 91–92, 104–107
Plot summary, 91
Plurals, 18, 55
Poetry:
  essay about, 91–94
  how to quote, 44, 94
  titles of, 45, 92–93
Possessive nouns and
    pronouns, 18
Prefixes and Suffixes, 11–13
Prewriting (see Planning)
Pronouns:
  agreement (singular and
    plural), 19–21
  case (*I* and *me*), 22–23
  he/she, 20, 138
  I, 20, 22–23
  me, 22–23
  possessive, 18
  reference, 19–21, 24–25

Pronouns (Cont.):
  sexism and, 20, 138
  they, 19, 21
  vague, 24–25
  you, 21
Proofreading, 80–81, 87–90
Punctuation marks:
  apostrophes, 18
  colons, 38
  commas, 35–36
  dashes, 39
  exclamation points (in
    quotations), 42
  hyphens, 10
  parentheses, 39–40
  periods, 26–34
  question marks (in
    quotations), 42
  quotation marks, 41–44
    vs. underlining, 45
  semicolons, 33, 37, 143

Quotation marks, 41–44
  with titles of works, 45
Quoting (using quotations),
    41–44, 95–96
  dialogue, 43
  indenting long quotations,
    42–43
  in literature essays, 41–44,
    92–96
  poetry, 44
  punctuation before and after,
    41–42
  in research papers, 95–96,
    106, 108, 109–117

Racist language, avoiding, 137–138
Reading:
  writing about, 91–94
Redundancy, 139
Repetition, avoiding, 139
Research papers, 97–125
  bibliography for, 118–125
  documentation, 112–115
  footnotes and endnotes, 112
  ideas for, 104–105
  library, use of, 97–100, 103
  organization of, 107–108
  parenthetical citations, 112–117
  plagiarism in, 106, 111
  work cited, 118–125
Revision, 68–71, 147
  of conclusions, 72, 74
  of introductions, 72–74
  of paragraphs, 75–77
  of sentences:
    choppy, 143–144
    varying, 142–146
    wordy, 139–141
  using transitions, 78–79
  of wordiness, 139–141
Run-on sentences, 33–34, 142–144

s and *'s* endings, 18, 54, 56
Semicolons, 33, 37, 143
Sentences:
  awkward, 24–25, 56–58
  choppy, 143–144
  complete, 26–28
  complex, 28
  compound, 27
  dangling modifiers in, 57

Sentences (Cont.):
  faulty, 56–58
  fragments, 26–30, 39, 142–144
  mixed patterns in, 58
  run-on, 33–34, 142–144
  simple, 26–27
  subordinate, 28
  topic, 66, 68, 77, 88–89, 104, 107
  variety in, 142–146
  wordiness in, 139–141
Sexist language, avoiding, 20, 137–138
Sources:
  bibliography of 118–125
  crediting, 94, 111–117
  electronic, 98–103, 114–115, 120–121
  how to cite, 112–117
  how to quote from, 95–96
  when to identify, 111–112
Spacing:
  indenting paragraphs, 75
  in typing, 85–86
Specific writing, 133–134
Spelling, 11–13
  and abbreviations, 16
  capitalization, 14–15
  commonly confused words, 3–7
  i before *e*, 11
  numbers, 16–17
  word endings, 11–13, 18, 46–53, 54–55
Style:
  adding details, 133–134
  avoiding biased language, 137–138
  dramatic order, 144–145

Style (Cont.):
  finding your voice, 132
  fixing choppy sentences,
    143–144
  recognizing clichés, 135–136
  trimming wordiness, 139–141
  varying sentences, 142–146
Subject (see Topic)
Subject-Verb agreement, 53
Subordination (sentence
    patterns), 28–31, 144
Summary, 91, 109, 112

Tenses of verbs; (see Verbs,
    tenses)
Term papers (see Research
    papers)
Tests, essay, 88–90
Their, there, they're, 6
Thesaurus, use of, 103
Thesis statement, 66, 68, 77,
    88–89, 104, 107
Titles, 45, 92–93
  capitalization of, 14–15
  creating a title, 92
  italicizing or underlining
    of, 45
  punctuation of, 38, 45, 92–93
  quotation marks for, 45
  on cover sheet, 45, 86–87
To, too, two, 6
Topics:
  first ideas about, 61–64, 91
  for journal entries, 129–131
  paragraph development of,
    75–77
  what to do when you're
    stuck, 61–64
Transitions, 78–79
Typing your paper, 85–87

Underlining, titles of work, 45

Vaguenes:
  adding details, 133–134
  developing paragraphs, 75–77
  in pronouns, use of, 24–25
  when to make a paper
    longer, 70
  wordiness, 139–141
Verbs:
  active, 140–141
  agreement with nouns
    (singular, plural), 53
  auxiliary, 46–49, 51–52
  being verbs, 46–50, 140–141
  endings of, 46–55
  helping verbs, 46–49, 51–52
  infinitives, 31–32, 48
  -ing verbs, 12, 31, 46, 48, 53
  passive, 140–141
  tenses, 46–54
    future, 48
    in literature essays, 51, 94
    of irregular verbs, 49–50
    past, 47
    present, 46, 53
    shifting, 51–52
  with *to*, 31–32, 48
  Voice in writing, 132

Which, 24
Who, 7, 23, 25
Word division, 86
Word endings, 11–13, 18, 46–53,
    54–55
  -ed, 11, 47, 51, 54
  -ing, 12, 31, 46, 48, 53

-ly, 13
-*s* and -'*s*, 11–12, 18, 46, 53, 55
Wordiness, trimming, 139–141
Words:
    abstract and concrete, 133
    dividing at line endings, 86
    tone of, 132
Works cited:
    form of, 118–125
    sample page for, 124–125

World Wide Web, 100–101
Would, 50, 53
Writer's block, 61–64
Writing process, vii–viii, 61–71

You, 21